# Talking Donald Trump

*Talking Donald Trump* examines the language of Donald Trump's presidential campaign from the perspective of sociocultural linguistics. This book offers an insight into the many stages of Trump's political career, from his initial campaign for the Republican nomination, up to his presidency. Drawing from speeches, debates, and interviews, as well as parodies and public reactions to his language, Sclafani explores how Trump's language has produced such polarized reactions among the electorate. In analyzing the linguistic construction of Donald Trump's political identity, Sclafani's incisive study sheds light on the discursive construction of political identity and the conflicting language ideologies associated with the discourse of leadership in modern US society. *Talking Donald Trump* provides a crucial contemporary example of the interaction between sociolinguistics and political science, and is key reading for advanced students and researchers in the fields of sociolinguistics, language and politics, communication studies and rhetoric.

**Jennifer Sclafani** is Associate Teaching Professor of Linguistics at Georgetown University, USA. She has also been on the faculty at Hellenic American University in Athens, Greece, since 2009.

# Talking Donald Trump
A Sociolinguistic Study of Style, Metadiscourse, and Political Identity

**Jennifer Sclafani**

Routledge
Taylor & Francis Group

LONDON AND NEW YORK

First published 2018
by Routledge
2 Park Square, Milton Park, Abingdon, Oxon OX14 4RN

and by Routledge
605 Third Avenue, New York, NY 10017

First issued in paperback 2020

*Routledge is an imprint of the Taylor & Francis Group, an informa business*

*British Library Cataloguing-in-Publication Data*
A catalogue record for this book is available from the British Library

*Library of Congress Cataloging-in-Publication Data*
A catalog record for this book has been requested

ISBN 13: 978-0-367-73595-1 (pbk)
ISBN 13: 978-1-138-24450-4 (hbk)

Typeset in Times New Roman
by Apex CoVantage, LLC

# Contents

# Illustrations

**Figures**

**Tables**

# 1 Language and political identity

## Analyzing presidential language

On July 21, 2016, the real estate mogul, entrepreneur, and reality television star Donald Trump received the official nomination to become the Republican Party's candidate for the 2016 US presidential election. A newcomer to the national political scene, and considered one of the most (if not the most) rhetorically unconventional, controversial, and divisive candidates in US presidential history, Mr. Trump's road to the Republican nominating convention was followed by the news media as closely as many followed his popular reality television show, *The Apprentice*.

Donald Trump became famous, and infamous, not so much for his political stances, which were rarely expressed in any detail during his primary campaign. It was rather *how* he expressed his stances linguistically that fascinated pundits and the public alike. The language of Donald Trump – at the time of writing, President Trump – has been the subject of much debate, both in terms of the rhetorical style in which he has delivered criticism of various individuals and groups, and what some have referred to as the candidate's general oratorical lack of coherence and substance.

It is not the case that Mr. Trump was the first American presidential candidate in history to have received criticism for his oratorical skills or lack thereof. In recent presidential history, President George W. Bush became known for his "folksy" style and awkward diction. In fact, as Lim (2008) has documented, presidential rhetoric has been considered to be on a downhill path since the birth of the nation. However, the presidential candidacy of Donald Trump has brought studies on the declining discourse of American presidential figures into the mainstream media limelight over the past two years, and has even spurred new studies and commentary in academic and journalistic circles. Scholars of language and gender have weighed in on the sexism and misogyny (e.g., Cameron, 2016; Lakoff, 2016 [February 6]; Tannen, 2016) prevalent in his speech; others have homed in on Trump's racist discourse (e.g., Murphy, 2016; Schwartz, 2016).

However, the majority of coverage of Donald Trump's language throughout the 2016 election season, and especially during the primaries, focused less on meaning and more on the candidate's lack of stylistic finesse and linguistic complexity. For example, a *Boston Globe* study that received a great deal of attention during the primaries performed a comparative analysis of the grade level of presidential candidates based on transcripts of their candidacy announcements and found that the complexity of Donald Trump's language equaled that of a fourth grader, earning him the lowest score of 19 Republican and Democratic candidates analyzed (Viser, 2015). The author of the study also cites other nonpartisan studies that have documented a decline in complexity in presidential speech throughout the course of history based on analyses of other types of discourse, including State of the Union speeches and congressional speeches.

It is important to point out that the *Globe* study employed the Flesch-Kincaid algorithm to determine the average grade-level readability of political speeches, which, when compared with other similar studies, provides us with a seemingly robust quantitative comparison of presidential rhetorical styles from both synchronic and diachronic perspectives, but leaves unexplored many of the questions that interest sociolinguists and discourse analysts when approaching questions about language use in political discourse. One of the differences in the way that sociolinguistically informed discourse analysis differs in its approach from the aforementioned studies has to do with the keen attention paid to contextual factors influencing the speech event. For instance, the Flesch-Kincaid algorithm used in the *Globe* study and others is a test developed to analyze the difficulty of *written* discourse, but it was applied to *spoken* speeches. A wealth of literature in sociolinguistics (see Chafe & Tannen, 1987; Chafe, 1994 for an overview) has described in great detail a number of key differences between spoken and written discourse, taking into account both cognitive and social factors. The acknowledgment of the numerous differences between spoken and written language renders any study using metrics developed to analyze written texts on spoken discourse highly problematic, especially when making claims that implicitly postulate cognitive "deficiency" of the speaker by comparing scores of written speech to grade-level reading development. While the "deficit" reading of these studies cannot be attributed to the publications themselves (i.e., the assumption that because Trump speaks at a fourth-grade reading level, he is cognitively incapable of higher order thinking), they were immediately seized upon by media outlets around the globe and were clearly interpreted through a deficit lens.

A second reason that it is worthwhile to reconsider the speech of presidential candidates from the perspective of sociolinguistically informed discourse analysis is that algorithmic studies tend to overlook discourse-level features that play an important role in structuring spoken discourse, like repetition and syntactic parallelism, which are common rhetorical strategies that make spoken discourse not only *easier* to digest (in a cognitive sense) but also more *pleasant* (in a poetic sense) and *engaging* (in a social sense). Linguists have touched on some of these strategies in blogs and mainstream newspaper op-eds, taking a variety of analytic perspectives. For example, Donald Trump's extensive use of repetition has been described as a substitute for substantive explanations (Lakoff, 2016 [April 6]) or as a technique to strengthen hearers' neural circuitry and beliefs about candidates' attributes (G. Lakoff, quoted in Rossman, 2017).

While the type of polyfunctionality associated with repetition and parallelism just described relates to different types of audience appeal, we can also consider polyfunctionality as it relates to the construction of discourse coherence. Given that one of the most frequent evaluations of Donald Trump's speech is that it lacks coherence, this is a feature that will be considered in depth in this book. Additionally, the algorithmic studies described earlier have not analyzed textual cohesion and its role in the construction of coherence, which are characteristics of a text that rely in part on the use of small, seemingly simple (often one-syllable) words, commonly referred to as pragmatic or discourse markers. Discourse markers have been shown to play important and complex roles in the construction of textual coherence (e.g., Fraser, 1999; Jucker & Ziv, 1998; Schiffrin, 1987), and their role in governing the sequential and hierarchical relations among propositions in a text cannot be quantified by a simple algorithm. This last point is important and especially relevant to the present study given that one of the most common evaluations of Donald Trump's spoken discourse is that it is incoherent.

## Origin of the book

The ideas and analysis presented in this book represent in part the notes I have gathered throughout the past year and half, both in my role as a Washington, DC-based linguist with a background in qualitative discourse analysis and in my role as a participant observer of the American political process. I tend to follow politics with multiple hats on, whether I'm watching a televised debate, press conference, or campaign speech. One hat relates to my role as an engaged citizen and voter, in which I digest political media to inform myself about the candidates, their proposed policies, and the current events that affect my local, national, and global communities. A second hat that I bring to my engagement with political media is as an inhabitant of the

Washington, DC, metro area. When I first moved to Washington to attend graduate school, I quickly became aware that in a city where so many people's livelihoods revolve around national politics, keeping up with politics is akin to keeping up with the Red Sox in my hometown of Boston: whether or not you have any interest in baseball, you need to have some idea how the team is doing to get yourself through the day, since small talk about the Red Sox surfaces as frequently as the weather in other parts of the United States. In other words, staying current with political events is an essential part of one's communicative competence in many Washington social circles whether or not one's professional work is directly related to politics. National political news is important to Washington residents in other ways as well, given that non-federal employees' work lives are impacted by the goings on of the federal government as well. For instance, those who work in the hospitality and services industry were negatively financially affected by the partial federal government shutdown of 2013. On the other hand, DC commuters noticed some relief in the rush-hour traffic flow.

A third hat I bring to this analysis, and the one most important to the study of the language of Donald Trump, is my training in interactional sociolinguistics and discourse analysis with a focus on the discursive construction of identity. My interest in language and identity was not originally political in nature, but focused on language and the construction of regional, ethnic, and gender identities. A parallel area of research I have been involved in over the past decade is the sociolinguistic study of style, which is where I first began examining the language of Donald Trump and where I first became interested in following politics from a sociolinguistic perspective. In 2006, I followed the Washington, DC, mayoral campaign of Adrian Fenty, analyzing his use of phonological features of African American English in different speaking contexts and considering how audience, frame, and setting contributed to his relative use of the vernacular. At the same time, I began a concurrent project on gender, leadership, and sociolinguistic style, and spent time comparing the language of Donald Trump and Martha Stewart, who at the time both served as hosts of the reality television show, *The Apprentice*. I became interested in the ways that Trump's trademark leadership linguistic style was embraced and altered by Stewart in her role as a female executive. For example, Donald Trump's original trademark line of dismissal – "You're fired!" – was expressed in softer, mitigated terms characteristic of stereotypical "Women's Language" (Lakoff, 2004[1973]) by Stewart, such as "You just don't fit in" or "I wish you well, but I'm going to have to say good-bye."

Though it was not the focus of my early studies on gender and leadership style, in retrospect, it is fair to say that Donald Trump's language on *The*

*Apprentice* could be characterized as stereotypically hypermasculine, with unhedged, "bald on-record" (Brown & Levinson, 1987) face-threatening statements. In the context of *The Apprentice*, one could argue that Donald Trump's style should be taken as the established norm, since he was the executive producer and star of the original series. By contrast, a decade later, and in an entirely different leadership context, his "presidential" linguistic style, which in many ways does not differ substantially from his reality television style, is now viewed as markedly distinct from any type of discourse we might think of as a "presidential" norm.

In 2011, I taught a course entitled Language and Identity at Georgetown University, which coincided with the 2012 GOP primary cycle. My students and I were all engrossed in the extensive coverage of the Republican race, and with 11 nationally televised debates occurring over the course of one semester, we often turned to this readily available data for examples of the discursive phenomena we were studying in class. At this time, I began examining the Republican primary debate discourse more systematically, focusing on features such as how candidates introduced themselves (Sclafani, 2015), how they managed to refocus their responses to moderator questions through the use of discourse markers (Sclafani, 2014), and how they used narrative-grounded constructed dialogue to portray themselves as powerful yet relatable characters (Sclafani, 2012a).

When a new election cycle began in 2015, I was curious to see whether candidates – and especially Republicans, since I had a direct point of comparison – would follow the same patterns I had observed in the previous race. As the Republican primary debates began in the late summer of 2015, I was struck equally by how similar the majority of the GOP candidates' strategies were to the data I had previously analyzed as I was struck by the extent to which Donald Trump's style contrasted with these established patterns. I also began following with interest the mainstream media coverage of the primaries, noticing how much coverage was devoted to elusive identity-oriented characteristics of presidential candidates, like "authenticity" and "conviction" and "likeability." Donald Trump stood out in terms of these qualities from the historically large number of Republican candidates polling well enough to earn spots in the early debates (17 candidates participated in the first debate on August 6, 2015), coming out as the "authenticity" candidate of the Republican Party (Sargeant, 2015) going into the early primaries and caucuses, earning more favorable ratings than his Republican opponents throughout the majority of the primary season (Real Clear Politics, 2016) and eventually earning the party's official nomination after gaining over 13 million popular votes, the most of any GOP nominee in history (Bump, 2016). However, as political analysts have pointed out, Trump also received more votes *against* him (i.e., votes for all the other GOP candidates combined) than any candidate in history, making him, in terms of voter turnout, arguably the most divisive primary candidate in US electoral history.

Given both these record voting numbers and findings from political communication research showing that voters tend to vote according to personality traits like "likeability" and authenticity" rather than a candidate's experience or policy positions (e.g., Aylor, 1999; Hacker, 2004; Miller, Wattenberg, & Malanchuk, 1986), it is well worth taking an in-depth look at how Donald Trump discursively constructs a presidential image for himself during his campaign. Any reader that has even glanced at American political news headlines in 2016 may be scratching their head when I frame questions about the language of Donald Trump in terms of qualities associated with "likeability." How can a man who has insulted so many individuals and groups have any qualities associated with the sense of likeability? The problem is that "likeability" is sometimes erroneously equated with "niceness." It is clear that Donald Trump was by no means nice in any sense of the word during his presidential campaign, nor did he try to be. He blatantly insulted and attacked individuals and groups of every background and status on a nearly daily basis for over a year, and despite his repeated vows to "be more presidential" as his primary campaign came to an end and he transitioned into the general election season, his style has remained essentially the same up until the time of writing, in the early stages of his first term as US president.

So we must ask, despite a consistent display of a straightforwardly nasty persona, why was Trump considered so likeable as a candidate? Robin Lakoff (2000, 2005) has addressed the question of "Niceness"[1] in politics in detail, grounding her discussion of perceptions of what counts as "Niceness" in the political world amidst the increasing erosion of the distinction between the public and private sphere:

> Whether in the political or the entertainment arena, as citizens or fans we increasingly want to see, and insist on interpreting, public figures as private friends or family members, looking to their public performances for indications about their private selves and personalities. Increasingly we expect their utterances to sound unrehearsed and off-the-cuff, and increasingly their image consultants, spin-meisters, and speechwriters oblige. Even though on one level most of us are aware that what we are seeing is not the off-the-cuff discourse of daily intimacy, many of us persist in reading it as if it were, and judging its producers by the same principles we use for assessing the characters of people in our intimate lives.
> (Lakoff, 2005, p. 174)

Lakoff connects the privatization of public discourse not only with the rise of the mass media but also with the ascension of women in the public sphere in the late twentieth century and the accommodation of public discourse to admittedly stereotypical understandings of women's preferences for particular genres and styles of public discourse, which she claims is a source of the rise of the mixed genre of infotainment.

While the connection between gendered discourse and the importance of niceness in the political world may seem irrelevant to a discussion about the nastiness of a male politician, I hold that the gendered nature of niceness and nastiness are not only complementary but also part and parcel of the same phenomenon. As Lakoff remarks, on the one hand, we may assume that expectations regarding polite behavior of men and women in the public sphere converge as gender roles converge in society. However, "if at the same time as roles are apparently converging, there is a strong if unspoken conservative pressure to restore the old dichotomy, we may find ourselves in a complex and ambiguous situation" (p. 178). Indeed, in 2016, with the first woman winning a major party nomination for the American presidency, the unspoken pressure to "restore the old dichotomy" has risen to the surface in political discourse in rather straightforward terms. And it is of course not only evolving gender norms that precipitated the rise of a candidate like Donald Trump; the rise of right-wing populism as a backlash to the political and economic forces of globalization around the world has been widely documented by other social scientists (e.g., Wodak, 2015). Even if the social structures of these "old dichotomies" that Lakoff refers to are sometimes left underspecified in terms like "America" on campaign slogans, we find them clearly articulated in the discourse of Donald Trump's campaign and in the talk of his supporters.

As Lakoff (2005) documents the rise of Nice in politics, she cites Ronald Reagan, Bill Clinton, and George W. Bush as exemplifying Nice personae through appeals to approachability, folksiness, informality, and emotionality, as opposed to candidates like Bob Dole, Al Gore, and John Kerry, who were widely perceived as distant and aloof elitists. When factoring gender into the equation, Lakoff claims that while the connection between Niceness and masculinity are straightforward in political discourse, the connection with femininity is problematic (p. 182) because of the double bind for women in leadership roles (Jamieson, 1995; Lakoff, 2004[1973]) in which "nice" and "powerful" are mutually exclusive character traits for a woman to aspire to project in the public sphere.

While Lakoff's discussion of Niceness predates Hillary Clinton's first presidential bid, much has been written about the double bind as it relates to the presidential candidacies of Clinton in both scholarly outlets and the mainstream media (e.g., Lim, 2008; Meeks, 2012; Romaniuk, 2016; Sclafani, in press; Tannen, 2016) regarding the gender stereotype challenges she faces, the media coverage of her campaign, and her discursive strategies for straddling the competing needs to project authority and likeability. Given the rising prominence of niceness over the past couple decades in American political discourse, one might expect a nice GOP candidate to have prevailed in the 2016 primaries. However, among 17 candidates, the *least* nice of all prevailed as the most likeable. This may be due to what Lakoff (2005) predicted: the clash between gender convergence in the public sphere and growing conservative pressures to restore traditional norms have resulted in an ambiguous and complex situation that has given rise to a "No More Mister Nice Guy" momentum based on a slightly modified throwback to a pre-Nice era of hegemonic masculinity (see e.g., Brooks, 2016).

With this background in mind, we come to the central questions that this book addresses: What, exactly, does Donald Trump do through language in his public appearances throughout the primary season to create an "authentic" and "relatable" presidential persona among the field of GOP candidates? How does he manage to pass a "likeability" test despite his consistent nastiness? How does he distinguish his brand among the 16 candidates against whom he is vying for the nomination? In order to answer these questions, I will first utilize tools of a sociolinguistically informed discourse analysis to highlight elements of Trump's style that set him apart from his primary opponents and analyze the functions of these strategies. However, questions about Trump's language and its effectiveness in his primary campaign must go beyond his distinctive style to include at least some consideration of the provocative and inflammatory content of his talk, especially as it has related to women, Muslims, minorities, people with disabilities, and his personal attacks on other candidates, media figures, and various others. This will be done through an analysis of metadiscursive commentary about his language throughout the campaign.

Third, keeping in mind the interactional, co-constructed nature of identity, the intense amount of talk *surrounding* Trump's language cannot be underestimated. Thus, I also consider how the language of Donald Trump is taken up and contextualized in the media. The increase in the amount of metadiscourse surrounding the 2016 presidential election can be attributed in part to the increased number of channels of political media discourse. While social media microblogging platforms like Twitter did play a role in the previous election cycle (Conway, Kenski, & Wang, 2013; Evans, Cordova, & Sipole, 2014), media critics have pointed out the possibility that Twitter hadn't yet reached its full potential in 2012, speculating that 2016 would be considered the "Twitter" election (Kantrowitz, 2012). Indeed, the use of Twitter and other social media platforms (e.g., Snapchat) has reached new levels, and has been the source of a large amount of metadiscourse surrounding the language of Donald Trump's campaign.

This metadiscourse takes many forms: news reports highlighting controversial remarks made by the politician in speeches and debates, op-eds and commentaries from professional debate coaches analyzing Trump's unconventional rhetorical strategies, round-table style political talk shows analyzing the candidate's political strategies potentially encoded in his language, parodic impersonations on late-night talk shows, various types of social media quoting in the form of retweets, memes, etc. Metadiscourse surrounding Donald Trump's language via Twitter doesn't stop at the content or style of his language alone, but has further extended to commentaries on the time of day he tweets, the frequency of his posting, and his use of images on social media. The style of Donald Trump's tweets, which tends to mirror his spoken discourse, has even become the subject of a variationist study itself. Data scientist David Robinson (n.d.) found systematic differences in the language of tweets posted by Trump himself versus his campaign staffers (determined by the device from which they originated) and observed, for example, that Trump voices "angrier" tweets than other staffers who animate him on Twitter.

It would be overly simplistic to assert that the unconventional language of Donald Trump's style alone has generated the unprecedented amount of metadiscourse in the mainstream mass media and social media in 2015–2016. However, the amount of talk about language generated by his primary campaign cannot be ignored and points to latent language ideologies about leadership, identity, and what Hill (1995) has described as the "leaky" boundary between the public and private spheres.

## A discourse analytic approach

In her nomination acceptance speech at the 2016 Democratic National Convention, Hillary Clinton made the following remark about Donald Trump:

> At first, I admit, I couldn't believe he meant it either. It was just too hard to fathom – that someone who wants to lead our nation could say those things. Could be like that. But here's the sad truth: There is no other Donald Trump. This is it.

What Clinton says here in many ways articulates the theoretical framework underlying the analysis in this book: in the world of politics, *you are what you say*. Every speech, every interview response, every conversation, and every tweet culminates in an image of a political persona that voters must evaluate against other personae, and, ultimately, a persona that they must vote for or against at the ballot box. As Silverstein (2003a) remarked in his book about the linguistics of presidential style, it is fallacious to separate a politician's substance and style; rather, in the world of politics, substance *is* style. Silverstein (see also Lempert & Silverstein, 2012) also contends that from this perspective, the "message" is not the theme or the point of political communication, but it is the ideological space inhabited by the communicator him or herself. The erasure of the distinction between the person and their words, at least within the realm of public political figures, calls for a discussion of how semiotic links are made between language and speaker identity, and how certain linguistic forms become enregistered (Agha, 2005, 2007; Silverstein, 2003b) as emanating from certain types of social personae.

These connections can be uncovered through a sociolinguistically grounded discourse analytic study of language by and surrounding the primary campaign of Donald Trump. The most important assumption underlying a discourse approach is that all language use is grounded in and simultaneously creates multiple layers of social context. A common definition of discourse analysis is the study of linguistic structure "above and beyond the sentence" (Schiffrin, 2014). Language "above" the sentence refers to units that extend beyond the syntactic clause, which is the major unit of analysis in the study of formal syntax. A discourse-level unit may thus be a paragraph in a written text, a turn in a conversation, or a personal narrative in a formal speech, all of which usually contain multiple clauses. On the other hand, language "beyond" the sentence refers to the importance of social context. Aspects of context that are taken into account include the roles and identities of speakers and hearers in a conversation; the physical, institutional, and social setting of the talk; the communicative mode; and the goals and purposes of the language – which, in political discourse, may be to persuade, inform, entertain, or a combination thereof. Johnstone (2008) defines the role of the discourse analyst as the following:

> We are not centrally focused on language as an abstract system. We tend instead to be interested in what happens when people draw on the knowledge they have about language, knowledge based on their memories of things they have said, heard, seen, or written before to do things in the world.
>
> (p. 3)

Following this conceptualization of discourse analysis, the analysis in this book focuses on how the language of Donald Trump draws on underlying shared knowledge and expectations about how language works, and how it is connected to our understanding of people as particular social types, in order to construct an identity for himself that matches a social type that voters believe would best represent a leader of the Republican Party and the nation.

Several models of discourse structure have been proposed to study the structure of language above and beyond the sentence from various sub-fields of linguistics, such as pragmatics (e.g., Polanyi, 1988) and computational linguistics (e.g., Mann & Thompson, 1988). I will employ Schiffrin's (1987; Maschler & Schiffrin, 2015) model of discourse structure because it accounts for social interactional aspects, formal cohesive properties of discourse structure, and considerations of the cognitive states of participants in the construction of conversational coherence. Briefly, Schiffrin posits five planes or levels of discourse structure. First, the "exchange structure" of discourse relates to the organization of turn taking and floor exchange in multiparty discourse. Considerations at this level relating to the language of Donald Trump would include issues such as the type, frequency, and function of interruption in debate and interview contexts. Second, the "act structure" of discourse relates to all aspects of the performance of speech acts: which speech acts are prevalent in a text and through what modes – direct or indirect, which forms of politeness – are they accomplished. At this level, we might consider how Donald Trump apologizes (or not) for past talk or actions, or the relative directness with which he issues declarations about his policy proposals at a rally.

A third level to consider is the "ideational structure" of talk, or the way in which propositions are organized within and across a text. At this level, we will consider Donald Trump's use of cohesive devices that link his current talk with his own and others' previous and upcoming talk. When he answers a question in a debate, for example, does he include language from the moderator's question to indicate explicitly his response as a response to the question asked? A fourth level at which we can analyze Donald Trump's idiosyncratic style is in terms of "information state," or the way his language use indicates assumptions about common ground and shared understandings of context between himself and his interlocutors, including both direct addressees (e.g., interviewers) and other ratified hearers (e.g., debate opponents, televisually mediated audiences). This consideration of audience relates to the fifth and overarching level described by Schiffrin, the "participation framework" of discourse. Participation framework involves all aspects of both speaking and hearing roles and identities in interaction, and how these are cued through talk. While the participation framework is always relevant to discourse coherence when one takes an interactional perspective to the analysis of political discourse, there are moments at which conscious attention to it can guide our understanding of how meaning is created through the other four levels. For example, when Donald Trump referred to an unflattering recording of himself making lewd remarks about his sexual interactions with (or rather, actions upon) women as an instance of "locker-room talk," he made reference to what is normally considered a private, nonserious, sex-segregated, and male-only genre of speech – that is, a genre associated with a highly specific participation framework – to relegate this to the private sphere of his life and excuse or exclude it as irrelevant to his public, political persona.

I will make use of this framework as I analyze the language of Donald Trump in order to answer the question of how he, in his role as a politician, uses language to actively construct a "presidential self" in discursive interaction. The study of social identity construction in discursive interaction lies at the foundation of the field of sociolinguistics (e.g., Gumperz, 1982) and has gained a robust representation within the field of sociolinguistics and linguistic anthropology over the past decade (e.g., Bucholtz & Hall, 2005; De Fina, Schiffrin, & Bamberg, 2006). The theoretical grounding of these and other studies on language and identity is articulated most succinctly in the work of Elinor Ochs (1992, 1993), who presents a language socialization perspective to the study of identity construction. Ochs employs the concept of indexicality to describe the way speakers and hearers construct links between particular linguistic forms and social qualities. According to Ochs, the indexical relationship between language and identity can be characterized by three qualities: it is 1) indirect, 2) constitutive, and 3) nonmutually exclusive.

Related to the notion of indirectness, Ochs explains that very few features of language directly index a social category. Taking gender as an example, in the English language, only pronouns like "he" and "she" and address titles like "Mr." and "Ms." directly and referentially index gender. Referential indexes of gender and other identities are far outnumbered by linguistic features that socially index identity. When they do so, the connection between language and identity is mediated via meanings associated with particular stances, speech acts, or activities. In this sense, the relationship between language and identity is said to be constitutive. Ochs uses the example of the sentence final particles "ze" and "wa" in Japanese, which are associated with the language of men and women, respectively. However, there is nothing inherently 'gendered' about these particles in the referential way that the pronouns "he" and "she" are gendered. Rather, they connote the affective stance of the speaker, with "ze" conveying a stance of coarse intensity with regard to the proposition in the sentence that it follows, while "wa" conveys gentle intensity. Because of dominant gender ideologies of masculinity and femininity and in Japan, the choice between these sentence-final particles constitutes gender identities through their indirect indexical relation to a certain affective stance.

The third relation described by Ochs – the nonmutually exclusive relation between language and identity – is perhaps the most important key in understanding how the language of Donald Trump has been so divisive throughout his campaign as a political figure and how he has come to be interpreted in such different ways by different audiences, with some viewing him as a strong, decisive, authentic leader and others viewing him has an incoherent and incompetent oaf. Ochs puts forth that very few linguistic features exclusively index a social category like gender. Instead, taking Japanese sentence-final particles again as an example, these features can be used by both men and women; that is, the use of sentence final "wa" doesn't *presuppose* that the speaker is a woman, but rather *suggests* it in a probabilistic way. A second facet of nonexclusivity has to do with the range of meanings that a linguistic feature may connote. For example, in English, final rising intonation on declarative sentences, sometimes referred to as "uptalk," is a feature that has long been associated with women, and especially with a stereotypical "Valley Girl" or bimbo type of female persona (but also young people more generally), but this feature has been demonstrated to index an array of meanings. Lakoff (2004[1973]) describes questioning intonation as connoting a particular epistemic stance – i.e., a lack of commitment or confidence in one's proposition. Guy and Vonwiller (1984) suggest a variety of interactional roles of final rising intonation, which may involve seeking verification of the listener's comprehension, negotiating a longer turn, or seeking the listener's reaction. With this "indexical field" (Eckert, 2008) sketched out for this individual feature, we may trace ways in which the use of questioning intonation could be used in ways that are consonant with dominant ideologies of femininity – i.e., by signaling a hesitant stance – but could also be used in ways that are consonant with ideologies of masculinity – i.e., as a power move to hold the conversational floor. In Chapters 2 and 3, as I sketch out some of the idiosyncratic features of Donald Trump's language throughout the primary campaign, I will focus on features that differentiate his talk from that of other candidates, as this distinction makes them salient and remarkable to his audiences, but as I do so, I will attempt to sketch out the multiple social meanings that are indexed by these features, which in turn allow for audiences to come away from the same speech with such different takes on what Trump's linguistic style means.

Current research in the field of sociocultural linguistics on language and identity has emphasized the situated, emergent, relational, and ideological aspects of individual and group identity construction, focusing on constructs such as "stance," "position," and "style" as a means for connecting micro-level linguistic strategies with mesolevel aspects of social engagement and macrolevel social structures (Bucholtz & Hall, 2005; Eckert & Rickford, 2001; Englebretson, 2007; Jaffe, 2009) in a similar fashion to the examples described in relation to Ochs's work. While much of this work has focused on how social constructs like ethnicity, gender, race, and sexuality are con-structed in discursive interaction, it has also given rise to a strong research interest in the construction of particular types of institutional roles and rela-tionships, like that of "teacher" and "student" in educational settings (see, for example, much of the research published in *Journal of Language, Iden-tity and Education*) or of "doctor" and "patient" in medical settings (e.g., Heritage & Clayman, 2010; Sarangi & Roberts, 1999). This study on the language of Donald Trump can also be considered an examination of the discursive construction of the institutional role of presidential candidate. Therefore, like any study of language and identity in an institutional setting, it must take into account the concept of power, which requires a consid-eration of the interaction between structure and agency, and how they both create and constrain the possibilities for identity construction. Bucholtz and Hall (2005) express this concern in what they call the "partialness princi-ple" of identity:

> On the one hand, it is only through discursive interaction that large-scale social structures come into being; on the other hand, even the most mundane of everyday conversations are impinged upon by ideo-logical and material constructs that produce relations of power. Thus both structure and agency are intertwined as components of micro as well as macro articulations of identity.
>
> (p. 605)

The current study can be viewed as a case study of language and identity at the institutional crossroads of politics and the media, which intersect in complex ways to create and constrain opportunities for the construction of political identities. In the American context of for-profit news corporations, certain individuals' political identities are ratified by the press, while oth-ers' may be essentially eclipsed. For example, in the presidential primaries, networks require that candidates hit certain polling numbers to participate in nationally televised debates. The media also has the power of selecting what speeches, debate clips, press conferences, and tweets to broadcast and replay. They also have the choice of which analysts they select to comment on political affairs. Such practices constrain the possibilities and power that candidates have over their discursive constructions of identity.

On the other hand, candidates may also act in ways to exert power over the media by speaking and acting in ways that are likely to earn them attention and airtime. Politicians' power over the media is of course also exerted financially through paid advertising, and as we have seen in the 2016 US presidential election, the negotiation of these power relations may even rise to the surface in the form of publicized feuds between politicians and the media. This has never been more apparent than in the candidacy of Donald Trump, who managed to run a campaign that, not surprisingly, bears some semblance to the drama and narrative arc of his reality television show. For instance, during his highly publicized feud with Fox News anchor Megyn Kelly, Trump announced he would boycott the January 28 Republican primary debate if she participated as a moderator, tweeting, "It will never happen. Fox will drop Kelly if it means no Trump. Nobody will watch w/o Trump" (@realDonaldTrump, Jan. 25, 2016). Mr. Trump did in fact skip the debate to hold a rally for Veterans and Wounded Warriors when Fox News announced that Kelly would continue to moderate the debate as planned. This could be considered a successful in this exertion of power for Trump, as the GOP debate received the second-lowest ratings of the season (Stelter, 2016).

While the issue of politics, power, and the media is an important one underlying the analysis I conduct in this book, I will take for granted the institutional effects and implications of the intersection of politics and the media for the majority of the book in order to highlight my central question: How is one individual's political identity constructed linguistically in the media, and how is this language taken up and interpreted by various audiences? This is not the first study to approach questions of this nature, so I will provide a brief summary of key findings in recent research on language and politics, highlighting how these approaches inform my own perspective and how the present study departs from prior analyses of the discursive construction of political identity.

Wodak's (2009) *The Discourse of Politics in Action* takes a critical perspective in analyzing the discursive basis of political identities and political action by performing an ethnography of the day-to-day work of Members of European Parliament (MEPs). Wodak grounds her trademark approach – the "discourse historical approach" – in identity-oriented concepts from interactional sociolinguistics, such as Goffman's (1959) distinction between "frontstage" and "backstage" identities and theorizing about professional socialization (e.g., Bourdieu, 1991; Lave & Wenger, 1991), and situates these within Foucauldian notions of power and discourse that shape and constrain identity performance. Wodak argues that this perspective allows for the analysis of how microlevel discursive interaction is affected by and how it shapes macrolevel institutional structures. She follows one MEP in his daily work, in both frontstage and backstage arenas, and complements this case study with a consideration of the media construction of politics via an analysis of the US television series *The West Wing*. While getting at the construction of political identity from these various angles, the vastly different contexts examined surrounding the language of politicians and the media portrayal of politics does allow readers to correlate these analyses with each other in order to get a holistic perspective on the interaction between the institutions of politics and the media. In the current study, I attempt to overcome this shortcoming by spending two chapters focusing on the distinctive language on one politician, and in the remaining analysis chapter, I examine interpretations of the same politician's language in the mass media in order to provide a full picture of the discursive performance, interpretation, and circulation of an individual's political identity.

Hodges (2011) zeroes in on discursive strategies employed in the discursive construction of the "War on Terror" in politics and the media following the events of September 11, 2001, closely following discourse in and surrounding the presidency of George W. Bush. Hodges's approach triangulates an analysis of Bush's speeches with an intertextual analysis of how this language was circulated and recontextualized in the media and among the American public via an analysis of a focus group discussion among college students. First, he shows through specific discursive phenomena like metaphor and historical analogy how President Bush creates a "war" narrative out of the events following September 11, employing language ideological and identity constructs like adequation (Bucholtz & Hall, 2005) and erasure (Gal & Irvine, 2000) to show how the American invasion of Iraq was construed as consistent with a goal of fighting the terrorist organization Al Qaeda. He also illustrates how laypeople with divergent political party affiliations take up and recontextualize media discourse as they talk about their own understanding of political issues in focus group contexts. Hodges's study is unique in its multi-tiered approach to examining the discursive constructions and interpretations of political meaning related to specific historical events and political actions. The current study attempts to triangulate in a similar manner regarding the discursive construction and perception of a specific political figure's identity.

Lempert and Silverstein (2012) build on and recapitulate the earlier individually authored work by the co-authors (e.g., Lempert, 2009, 2011; Silverstein, 2003a), examining the concept of "Message" in presidential politics, or the "biographical aura" (p. 100) that candidates build for themselves and that is built for them through media coverage. Message, for them, is akin to what I am calling identity and is multimodal, incorporating not only aspects of linguistic performance including lexicogrammatical features, phonological and prosodic structure, and textual poetics but also gesture, clothing, and staging. Their analyses focus on various elements of message-building, but each chapter relates to a different element and a different candidate, resulting in an in-depth but fragmented analysis of the discursive building blocks and mechanisms of political identity construction. In order to see how these aspects come together, the current study attempts to incorporate an analysis of primarily linguistic phenomena (but also some gestural features) and metadiscourse in the media surrounding the campaign of an individual candidate. Through this case study approach, readers can capture the push-pull relationship between politics and the media, between structure and agency, and between language and extralinguistic phenomena that work dynamically to construct an individual's political identity.

In sum, the works summarized here provide an important theoretical and methodological background to this study in their sustained focus to myriad linguistic features, discursive spaces, and sociopolitical and media contexts of political communication.

## What this book is (not) about

Given the amount of attention that the language of Donald Trump has already received in the mainstream media during the 2016 presidential election cycle, and that he continues to receive as US president, not only in America but around the world, as well as the timing of this study and the preconceptions that many readers will have coming into this book, it will be useful to begin this section by describing what this book is *not* about.

First, it should be emphasized that the analysis in this book focuses primarily on Trump's *primary* campaign and considers data beginning with his official announcement of candidacy on June 16, 2015, and ends with his official acceptance of the party's nomination at the Republican National Convention on July 21, 2016. Additionally, some data constituting metadiscourse of Trump will be drawn from the general election campaign, as this data continues to circulate, recontextualize, and resemiotize the linguistic and paralinguistic features that became enregistered and recognizable to his audiences during his primary campaign. While I consider how Donald Trump's language can be distinguished from all other primary candidates from both the Republican and Democratic parties, I focus primarily on how his linguistic style compares with the other Republican candidates against whom he was vying for the party's nomination. In my discussion of his linguistic style and construction of his presidential persona, I do not consider any of the candidate's speeches, appearances, or other statements that came out after his official nomination, at which point his campaign turned to focus primarily on defeating the Democratic nominee, Hillary Clinton. Likewise,

I do not include an analysis of his performance in the general debates or follow the controversies surrounding the emergence of the 2005 recording of the lewd remarks he made regarding sexual aggressions toward women, nor the allegations of his past sexual misconduct that surfaced weeks before the election, though I do provide this context in cases where metadiscourse surrounding Trump's campaign allude to these events. I also do not write about either his language, his work, or any controversies that surfaced during his tenure as president of the United States. The objective of this book is to understand how Donald Trump linguistically established himself as a viable presidential candidate from the position of a relative outsider to the American political sphere, how he capitalized on his outsider status, and how his distinctive linguistic style worked both for and against him in the eyes of the viewing public.

As described earlier, Donald Trump's language made headlines regularly throughout 2016, with reports usually focused on his inflammatory insults of other candidates and his "braggadocious" (to use Trump's idiolect) self-promotion. This book departs from the mainstream media coverage of his campaign in that I will be less concerned with the *content* and *targets* of his insults or the qualities of his self-praise. Instead, I focus on how such speech acts emerge in speeches and debates, and, specifically, how they are articulated linguistically, paying attention to specific discursive, grammatical, prosodic, and co-speech gestural patterns of articulation.

There was also much metadiscourse about the geographical characteristics of his (and Democratic contender Bernie Sanders's) native New York accent throughout the primaries, which other linguists have provided insight on in the mainstream media (e.g., Guo, 2016; Newman, 2015). While Trump's geographic origin as a New Yorker undoubtedly plays into his construction of identity, the social characteristics that interest me relate to discourse-level elements of his conversational style (Tannen, 2005) rather than phonological aspects of his idiolect. However, there are some instances I discuss in which phonological features associated with a New York accent do play a role in the construction of social identity – these come up chiefly in the discussion of parodies as metadiscourse about Trump's idiolect and not in the analysis of his style per se.

It should also be noted at the outset that this study is chiefly qualitative. I will not be applying algorithms like that of the Flesch-Kincaid studies described earlier to determine Donald Trump's grade level, IQ, or place on the narcissistic personality spectrum, though experts have weighed in on these matters elsewhere (e.g., Alford, 2015; McAdams, 2016; Nutt, 2016). Additionally, the qualitative analysis I provide in this book is not about whether Trump "actually means" what he says, nor is it a rhetorical evaluation of his style. At the core of this short book is a dispassionate, descriptive analysis of Donald Trump's linguistic style in various speaking contexts and a description of reactions to his style, and how his language is interpreted as indicative of his political identity as a presidential candidate. The perspective I take is rooted in sociocultural approaches to the study of language and identity, described earlier, which considers how language works to create interactional positions in discrete moments of interaction and how these culminate in the construction of stable social identities over time.

Considering the substantial amount of existing research in the field of sociolinguistics that approaches the study of the linguistic bases for social identity construction, and in particular, the language of political identities, one may wonder what useful knowledge a case study of Donald Trump's primary campaign could add to our current conceptualizations of the intersection between language, politics, and the media. In response, I argue that this study of an individual politician's speech across multiple contexts adds to our understanding of language and politics by looking at both consistency and variation in the use of particular discourse strategies across contexts like debates, speeches, and social and entertainment media. This study also departs from previous perspectives on language and politics by illuminating social perceptions of political language through an in-depth examination of political parodies as metadiscourse about a politician's idiolect.

The remainder of the book proceeds as follows. In the next two chapters, I discuss several aspects Donald Trump's discourse that set him apart from his opponents during the 2016 primaries and which distinguish him from other candidates in recent GOP primary history. Chapter 2 focuses on his idiosyncratic use of discourse-marking devices, while Chapter 3 investigates his use of interactional strategies including interruption, constructed dialogue, and co-speech gesture. Chapter 4 provides a linguistic analysis of popular late-night parodies of Donald Trump as a form of metadiscourse during his presidential campaign. While some parodies highlight elements of Trump's interactional style described in the preceding chapters, like his penchant for interruption or his direct refusals to respond to questions in debates, others highlight perceived inconsistencies in the content of his speech, especially surrounding remarks he made throughout his primary and general campaign that were perceived as sexist, racist, or xenophobic. Building on past sociolinguistic work on language, identity, and parodic high performance (e.g., Barrett, 2006; Coupland, 2007; Sclafani, 2009), the analysis examines how writers and performers of Trump parodies manipulate language to highlight Trump's style as an "indexical negative" (Sclafani, 2012b) of his political identity. Chapter 5 concludes by reflecting on and synthesizing the findings from the three analysis chapters, contextualizing the findings within research on stylistic variation and language ideologies, and discussing the implications of the findings for the fields of sociolinguistics and political communication. The book concludes by suggesting how the sociolinguistic study of political discourse benefits from detailed case studies of language by and about individual political figures, and suggests avenues for further research integrating perspectives on sociolinguistic style, metadiscourse, and political identity.

## Note

1   Lakoff (2005) capitalizes "Nice" and "Niceness." When I refer explicitly to her discussion of the concept, I will maintain the capitalization. When I use the term in the general sense, as a synonym for "likeable" and "likeability," I will use a lower-case "n."

# 2 Trump's idiolect

## Discourse-marking devices

## Introduction

This chapter, along with Chapter 3, examines several distinctive and frequently employed linguistic elements of Donald Trump's speech in the Republican primary debates and other public speaking events during his primary campaign. Building on sociolinguistic and anthropological perspectives on style in public and mediated discourse (e.g., Coupland, 2007; Eckert & Rickford, 2001; Hernandez-Campoy & Cutillas-Espinosa, 2012; Jaffe, 2009; Johnstone, 1996) and work from conversation and discourse analysis (e.g., Heritage & Clayman, 2010; Schiffrin, 1987; Tannen, 2007), the analysis focuses on salient stylistic elements of Trump's idiolect and compares them with other Republican candidates in the 2016 race as well as Republican primaries of the recent past.

The current chapter proceeds as follows: First, I provide some background on the analysis of sociolinguistic style in public discourse. Next, I describe the corpus of data selected for analysis. The analysis then considers several distinctive types of discourse-marking devices related to Donald Trump's style that are argued to perform several functions and contribute to the construction of his political identity in the 2015–2016 presidential primary season. I discuss these elements in the following order: (1) the use of turn-initial "well" (or rather, Trump's notable lack of use of this feature) as a preface to refocus responses to questions in dialogic contexts, (2) the use of "by the way" as a turn-medial marker of topic change, (3) the use of the phrase "believe me," and (4) other forms of epistrophic punctuation. Throughout the analysis, I draw comparisons and contrasts with prior analyses of politicians' speech (e.g., Duranti, 2006; Heritage & Clayman, 2010; Sclafani, 2015, in press). In conclusion, I discuss how these features, as well as others not considered in-depth here, contribute to the construction of a particular instantiation of a broader social type that I refer to as the "presidential self."

## Perspectives on style and identity

The study of speaker style has a long history in sociolinguistics, beginning with Labov's seminal work in New York City (1972), which identified style as a matter of contextually based intraspeaker variation that was considered to be dependent on the speaker's relative amount of attention paid to speech. Later approaches to stylistic variation expanded the potential factors affecting an individual speaker's style, taking into account audience factors (e.g., Bell, 1984; Rickford & McNair-Knox, 1994). In recent years, the study of style has been influenced by the so-called discursive-turn and third-wave perspectives (Eckert, 2012), and as a result, the concept of speaker agency and identity has come into focus when considering stylistic choices (e.g., Schilling, 2013; Schilling-Estes, 1998; Bucholtz & Hall, 2005). The latter approach, with a view toward speaker identity not just as an aggregate of demographic categories but as an ideological construct that not only influences but also is discursively constituted *by* stylistic language use informs the approach taken here. As opposed to earlier quantitative approaches to style that focused on an individual or social group's stylistic changes in different settings, with different audiences, and in different frames of interaction, recent approaches to style have also shifted to focus attention on the social indexicality of language (see Section 1.3 in Chapter 1) and on the constellation and selection of social meanings associated with both individual features and feature clusters within and across particular speaking contexts (Agha, 2007; Coupland, 2007; Eckert, 2000, 2008; Irvine, 2001; Silverstein, 2003b). At the same time, anthropological perspectives to style, which have focused on linguistic performance and genre (e.g., Bauman, 1978, 2000, 2008; Bauman & Briggs, 1990), have laid the important groundwork for current understandings of stylistic language use in explicitly public or "staged" performance contexts by highlighting the language ideological underpinnings, affordances, and constraints of stylistic choices (see Bell & Gibson, 2011 for an overview). Language ideologies and their implications for the discursive construction of identity are of direct import to this study because, as Irvine (2001, p. 22) puts it, the concept of style implicates a "system of distinction," where one particular style gains meaning in the way that it contrasts both with other possible styles and their corresponding social meanings.

Given that this study deals with an individual's style and how his language works toward the construction of a particular social identity – one that is "branded" (Lempert & Silverstein, 2012) and marketed to voters as emanating from an existentially coherent (Duranti, 2006) and readily identifiable individual or political self, I leave aside questions of intraspeaker variation that have been historically central to the study of the sociolinguistics of style and instead focus more on the concept of *style as distinction*. Specifically, I describe the ways in which Donald Trump's idiosyncratic style is produced and consolidated as a coherent form across various speaking contexts, how this style comes to be enregistered (Agha, 2007) or recognized as emanating from both a biographical individual and a social type, and how these linguistic features map onto a set of relatively stable, though possibly contradictory, social meanings associated with characteristics relevant to some viable (considering, in retrospect, that he won the Republican Party's nomination and the 2016 US presidential election) image of a contemporary American president.

In doing so, I rely on work in sociolinguistics that has dealt with the construction of linguistic individuals. Barbara Johnstone (1996) has written extensively about the intersection of rhetoric and linguistics in the language of self-expression in her book *The Linguistic Individual*. As Johnstone emphasizes in introducing this topic, the linguistic construction of the individual involves not just sociolinguistic descriptions of demographic and contextual factors and rhetorical explanations of purpose and audience, but requires psychological explanation, dealing with the ways people create and narrate selves as they are expressed in narrative (p. ix). Consistency, she argues, is key in creating a coherent self that is readily identifiable across various different speaking contexts (pp. 128–156). Through an examination of the late US Congresswoman Barbara Jordan's speech across more and less formal and edited spoken and written texts, she finds consistency in linguistic features such as the use of discourse markers, syntactic structures, pronoun choice, and informality markers (e.g., contractions). Johnstone also examines discursive devices that contribute to Barbara Jordan's consistent display of knowledge from a stance of moral authority, which, she argues, contributes to the construction of a particular type of political identity as well.

Homing in on the importance of the perception of style, Johnstone points out that identifications of a given idiosyncratic style rely in large part on repetition: "When a linguistic item is repeated, we attend to it for the same reason we attend to pattern in all our sensory media. If we did not, the world would be chaotic" (p. 176). While Johnstone links her analysis of the linguistics of individual expression to a broader understanding of language variation, choice, and change, her in-depth study can also be seen as a foundation for considering the discursive construction of political identity as a publically recognizable branded individual style.

In a study on the language of the lifestyle entrepreneur Martha Stewart and how her idiosyncratic style is manipulated in linguistic parody

(Sclafani, 2009), I have emphasized that when examining the language of public personalities – icons who have branded their identity across product lines, like Martha Stewart – we must depart from the variationist perspective that assumes that individuals change their linguistic style at various levels – from phonological to discoursal – and according to multiple layers of context, including audience, setting, purpose, and modes. Instead, in the analysis of public figures who have branded their identity for consumption, I have argued that we should expect, contrary to our expectations of ordinary speakers in everyday casual contexts, a greater degree of consistency across contexts. In the case of Martha Stewart, this involved employing similar styles of speech in her daytime television show, her guest appearances on late-night talk shows, her starring role in the spin-off of Donald Trump's reality television show *The Apprentice*, and in written texts featuring her voice in her magazine publications. In a similar fashion, Donald Trump must maintain linguistic consistency across the various spheres of his public appearances, including his transition from the world of business and reality television to his role in politics.

A main thrust of research that has come out over the past couple decades on discourse and identity has emphasized the co-constructed nature of identity in everyday contexts (e.g., De Fina, Schiffrin, & Bamberg, 2006; Georgakopoulou, 2007; Ochs, 1993). However, when we move from the realm of everyday conversational interaction to the mass mediatized realm of political discourse, it is also vital to take into account the ways in which production and perception are *filtered* in various ways. For an ethnographic understanding of the language and politics, an approach like that taken by Wodak (2009) is useful in that it captures both the frontstage and backstage talk within the political sphere. However, it is important to keep in mind that little of the talk behind closed doors that one can collect in an ethnography of politics (when a researcher is so lucky to gain access) directly reaches the public. On the one hand, we must consider that everything said by a politician – even in public contexts – is heavily edited in a variety of ways for mass consumption. This includes the editing of interviews for televised broadcast and the selection of quotations and soundbites for reproduction in print and broadcast journalistic reports. Even the camera angle during any televised event selects only certain nonverbal communicative information to broadcast while hiding other information. On the other hand, mass perception of a politician's language is also mediated via the mechanisms, institutional practices, and ideologies of political news reporting. For that reason, it is of ultimate importance to take metadiscourse surrounding Donald Trump's language into consideration. This topic will be addressed in detail in Chapter 4.

## Selection of data

Given the vast amount of campaign coverage and televised speaking events throughout Donald Trump's primary campaign that are available for analysis, I have selected a small but representative subset of debates and other public speaking events to discuss in this chapter. I have relied on video data of these events made available on YouTube and Donald Trump's official campaign website (www.donaldjtrump.com), which posts major public events and media related to the candidate, including debates, commercials, rallies, interviews, and other speeches throughout his campaign. I have also used the website of the American Presidency Project at the University of California at Santa Barbara (www.presidency.ucsb.edu) as a resource for debate transcripts, which have been downloaded and refined to reflect additional linguistic detail observed in the video recordings of the debates. When available, transcripts of other speeches examined were downloaded from news websites on which they aired and were further refined by the author.

Three of the 12 Republican prime-time primary debates have been chosen for the analysis in this chapter. Selection of these took into consideration the need for a representative selection with regard to (1) the temporal arc of the campaign; (2) possible differences in tone, structure, and style between debates hosted by different broadcasting companies and moderators; and (3) geographical effects. Table 2.1 outlines relevant information about the three debates chosen for this analysis.

I also chose four major formal speeches given by Trump throughout his primary campaign to examine in detail: his announcement of his candidacy (June 16, 2015), his official announcement of his vice-presidential running mate, Indiana Governor Mike Pence (July 16, 2016), and a speech he gave at the American Israeli Public Affairs Committee (AIPAC) Convention (March 21, 2016), an organization considered very important to gaining support in the Republican Party and one at which all presidential candidates were invited to speak. These speeches ranged in terms of content, audience, and style, with the AIPAC and acceptance speeches being read almost entirely from a teleprompter, while the candidacy announcement and running mate selection speeches appeared largely unscripted.[1]

## Analysis of discourse markers

When nonlinguists discuss the language of Donald Trump, both in the press and in everyday conversations about politics, they tend to focus on particular lexical items, such as the high frequency use of evaluative words

*Table 2.1* Selection of Republican primary debates.

| Debate number | Date | Host and moderators | Location | Participants |
|---|---|---|---|---|
| 1 | August 6, 2015 | Fox News: Bret Baier, Megyn Kelly, Chris Wallace | Cleveland, Ohio | Jeb Bush<br>Ben Carson<br>Chris Christie<br>Ted Cruz<br>Mike Huckabee<br>John Kasich<br>Rand Paul<br>Marco Rubio<br>Donald Trump<br>Scott Walker |
| 8 | February 6, 2016 | ABC News: David Muir, Martha Raddatz | Manchester, New Hampshire | Jeb Bush<br>Ben Carson<br>Chris Christie<br>Ted Cruz<br>John Kasich<br>Marco Rubio<br>Donald Trump |
| 12 | March 10, 2016 | CNN: Jake Tapper, Dana Bash, Hugh Hewitt, Stephen Dinan | Miami, Florida | Ted Cruz<br>John Kasich<br>Marco Rubio<br>Donald Trump |

like "huge," "stupid," and "disaster," and idiosyncratic phonological and suprasegmental patterns, such as Trump's New York accent and his emotionally charged "tone." Indeed, linguists have also investigated some of these features in the speeches of other US politicians (see Podesva, Hall-Lew, Brenier, Starr, & Lewis, 2012 and Hall-Lew, Coppock, & Star, 2010 for examples of regional accent analyses), and these particular features have undoubtedly distinguished Donald Trump from his Republican opponents during the 2016 primaries. However, following the framework I set up in the previous chapter, I will focus in this study on discourse-level phenomena that contribute at an interactional level to the construction of a political persona.

Discourse markers (DMs) are one such feature that plays an important role, and they have multiple functions at various planes of discourse. As outlined in Chapter 1, Schiffrin (1987, 2014) considers the role of DMs in the construction of discourse coherence, outlining how these words contribute to the structuring of discourse at each of the five planes of discourse coherence: participation framework, or aspects relevant to speaker and hearer identities and roles; exchange structure, or the turn-taking format of the discourse; action structure, or the performance of speech acts; ideational structure, or the structure of propositions and new and given information in a text; and information state, or the structuring of new and given information based on expectations about participation levels of knowledge and common ground in discourse. Other approaches to DMs, such as those grounded in relevance theory and pragmatics (e.g., Fraser, 1999; Jucker, 1993; Schourup, 1999), have also touched upon DM functions at certain levels outlined by Schiffrin, focusing on cognitive aspects like accessible context (Jucker, 1993) or pragmatic notions like the speaker's intention of highlighting cohesion with prior discourse (for a recent survey of DM research, see Maschler & Schiffrin, 2015).

### *Turn-initial "well"*

In my earlier research on discourse markers in presidential primary debates (Sclafani, 2014), I found that turn-initial DMs are frequently used in candidates' responses to moderators' questions and requests for rebuttals. In an analysis of a subset of the 2011–2012 Republican primary debates, DMs prefaced approximately one-third of all candidate responses (excluding direct responses to each other's attacks), with 31 percent of all responses featuring turn-initial "well." The four next most commonly employed turn-initial DMs markers combined ("you know," "look," "oh," and "now") accounted for only 6.5 percent of all candidate responses. It is unsurprising that "well" occurs so frequently in this context, considering its attested function in traditional DM analyses, which have pointed to its role as a reframing device, presupposition canceller, a face-threat mitigator, and an indicator of an indirect, insufficient, or disagreeing response (e.g., Jucker, 1993; Lakoff, 1973; Pomerantz, 1984; Svartvik, 1980; Watts, 1986).

More recent work has examined the frequency and function of "well" in specific genres of discourse. For instance, Norrick (2001) claims that "well" has specialized functions in oral narrative, marking transitions between distinct narrative sections and directing listeners back to the plot following digressions. Fuller (2003) finds that "well" occurs less frequently in interview contexts than in conversations, which she explains is due to the firmly established speaker roles within the participation framework associated with the interview genre, which is dominated by the question-answer format. In other words, in interviews, the interviewee is expected to be providing responses to the interviewer's questions, so the explicit marking of one's answers as responses via "well" is not necessary. As I have argued previously, Fuller's analysis would predict that "well" would not appear frequently in a debate format, which is also largely governed by a tightly moderated question-answer exchange structure. However, it seems that the agonistic genre of political debates and interviews, which are also governed by the expectation of critical, challenging questions, disagreement, and frequent question evasion (Clayman, 2001), provides a counterbalance to the pattern predicted by Fuller.

If we compare the overall distribution of discourse markers in the debates presently examined, we find a similar distribution of DMs overall, illustrated in Figure 2.1. As we can see, DM usage in the 2015–2016 debates resembles its distribution in 2011–2012, with "well" even more prevalent among turn-initial markers than in 2011–2012, prefacing 42% of all responses to moderator questions.

One question regarding discourse markers that has been made in passing (Sclafani, 2014; Tagliamonte, 2016) but has not received any straightforward

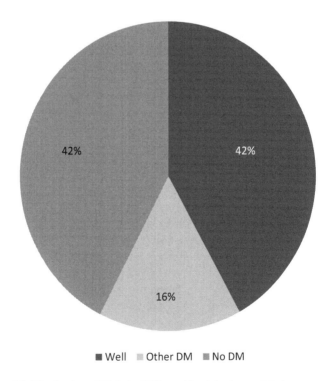

*Figure 2.1* Distribution of DMs in GOP presidential primary debates.

empirical investigation is whether DM usage may contribute to a particular individual's discursive style. Considering the attested usage of "well" in past presidential debates and common characterizations of Donald Trump's style as "brash," "direct," and "simple," it would be useful to see whether his choice and stylistic usage of DMs reflects this. Since analyses in the mainstream media have often commented on the relatively short length of his sentences compared to other presidential candidates, this may be a reflection of Trump's relatively infrequent use of DMs – and of "well" in particular, which may contribute to views of his discursive style as straightforward and unabashedly face-threatening.

In order to determine whether any stylistic differences in DM usage occur among the candidates, let us first examine the candidates' rate of use of DMs in the three debates in this corpus. Figure 2.2 displays the frequency with which each candidate prefaces his response with a DM. For simplicity and clarity, I have only included in these tabulations speakers who responded at least ten times throughout the three debates examined, which excludes candidates Huckabee, Paul, and Walker.

First, by looking at how frequently candidates preface their response with a DM, we can see that Trump, who is accorded far more opportunities to respond to moderators' questions overall (with 60 responses overall; Cruz

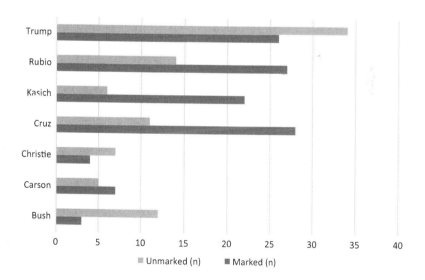

*Figure 2.2* Number of discourse-marked and unmarked debate responses by candidate.

is the next most frequent to respond, with 39 responses), responds *without* a turn-initial DM more frequently than he does with a DM (34 times without versus 26 times with a DM). Christie and Bush are the only other two candidates to be more likely to begin their responses without DMs, but given that they are accorded many fewer opportunities to respond overall in the debates, they have less of a chance for this pattern to "accrete" (Bucholtz & Hall, 2005) into perceivable discursive acts of social identity. Trump's high frequency of unmarked responses with common DMs (e.g., "well" or "you know") may contribute to a view of the candidate as a straightforward or decisive debater, given the attested role of "well" (and other DMs) in attenuating speaker stance.

Let us now examine the relative use of "well" as a turn-initial DM across the candidates in the debates in Figure 2.3. It has been observed that metadiscourse frequently follows the discourse marker "well" (e.g., Jucker, 1993; Lakoff, 1973; Sclafani, 2014). Common examples of metadiscourse in the debates are, "Well, let me begin by saying . . ." or "Well, let me break down the question." Such moves constitute explicit articulations by

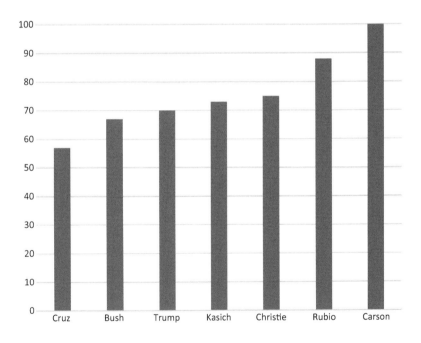

*Figure 2.3*  Percentage of turn-initial "well" in marked responses.

the candidates acknowledging the complexity of the moderator's question, and they can be thought of as an explicit display that the respondent is attempting to structure his response in order to comply with the moderator's request for a response.

Donald Trump, in conjunction with his relative lack of DMs, does not supply responses involving any type of metadiscourse. This distinction and stylistic choice can have multiple social meanings. First, it may be correlated with people's perceptions that Mr. Trump talks in a "decisive" or "straight-forward" manner. Connected to this indexical meaning, Trump's less frequent use of "well" may work toward the construction of the candidate as a political outsider by differentiating him from his potentially evasive opponents who frequently respond with "well . . ." On the other hand, taking into consideration the tendency of "well" as a preface to metadiscourse, it may also contribute to perceptions of his style as unaccommodating to the moderator. In other words, when other candidates use "well," it is an explicit acknowledgment that they are attempting to comply with the moderator by answering their questions (which frequently contain multiple propositions and subquestions) in full. In this sense, "well" may be argued to function as a politeness strategy that attends to the addressee's positive face (Brown & Levinson, 1987). Trump, by not using "well" frequently, may also be seen as not exploiting face-saving strategies, and instead answering questions using what Brown and Levinson refer to as a "bald, on-record" strategy in the performance of face-threatening acts.

Finally, if we consider the economy of words as an ideology underlying political discourse, one might correlate Trump's shorter and less hierarchically complex answers (due to the fact that he tends not to break them down into constituent parts prefaced by "well") as indexing a political persona who prefers less talk, potentially because excessive talk is thought of as an alternative to action. In fact, this language ideology is quite explicitly articulated elsewhere in Trump's speeches. On multiple occasions he has distanced himself from his opponents and politicians in general by saying they are "all talk, no action," while he has spent his life outside the political arena in the action-oriented field of business.

By taking a comparative look at which candidate exploits turn-initial "well" the most throughout the debates examined – Dr. Ben Carson – the argument regarding the contribution of this DM to perceptions associated with a speaker's overall "presidential self" becomes even more apparent. Carson, who maintained strong polling numbers early in the primaries, was known as the other major outsider among the Republican candidates, but he maintained a linguistic style that was very distinct from that of Donald Trump. Often referred to as "mild-mannered," "calm," and "soft-spoken,"

Carson's "tone" is described by Hamlin (2015) as softer and slower than the other candidates, which makes him sound "so reasonable, so thoughtful in his measured pronouncements." Hamlin argues that the indexical value of this linguistic style comes across to audiences as emanating from a candidate who carefully considers issues in advance and who is "reasonable" and "a clear-thinking, strong and unflappable leader, always in control." While Hamlin only refers to Caron's pacing and amplitude as indicators of his idiosyncratic style, it could be argued that his relatively high exploitation of turn-initial "well" also contributes to impressions of him as a candidate who reflects before speaking and who carefully considers all aspects of moderators' questions before answering in debates. Through this contrast between the two Republican outsider candidates, we have a clearer view of how Irvine's notion of "style as distinction" relates to the consideration of language in the context of political campaign discourse.

### *"By the way"*

Interestingly, while Donald Trump uses very few turn-initial DMs throughout the debates, there is one turn-medial discourse marker that he exploits to a greater extent than the other candidates: "by the way." This DM has been described as one that functions at the level of ideational structure, marking that an upcoming proposition is not related to the discourse topic (Blakemore, 2001; Halliday & Hasan, 1976; Schiffrin, 1987). Table 2.2 compares the use of this DM by candidates across the debates.

*Table 2.2* Occurrences of "by the way" by candidate in the three debates examined.

| Debate location | Candidate | Number of occurrences |
| --- | --- | --- |
| Cleveland | Trump | 4 |
| Manchester | Trump | 3 |
| | Kasich | 2 |
| | Rubio | 2 |
| | Christie | 1 |
| Miami | Trump | 8 |
| | Rubio | 2 |
| **TOTAL** | Trump | 15 |
| | Rubio | 4 |
| | Kasich | 2 |
| | Christie | 1 |
| | Carson, Bush, Cruz | 0 |

Trump's exploitation of the DM "by the way" is notable in that it is one of the few ways in which a candidate can steer the debate toward a topic of his/her own interest and be released from the constraint of having to comply with the topics selected by the moderators' questions. As Clayman (2001) has pointed out previously, "well" is a common turn-initial strategy for evading questions while "saving face" in the agonistic question-answer frame of broadcast interviews. But its salience due to its turn-initial position may be an obvious cue to audiences that the respondent is departing from the topic. The use of turn-medial "by the way," on the other hand, works to steer the topic of discussion in one's desired direction once the respondent already has the floor and has already established a flow to his or her answer.

Since there are so few instances of "by the way" in the corpus overall, we can examine them more closely to see how they are situated in context in order to better understand how Trump uses this marker as a discourse strategy in the debates. There is one lengthy exchange between Trump and moderator Chris Wallace in the Cleveland debate in which Trump utters "by the way" three times. I have reproduced this extract from the transcript that follows:

1  a WALLACE: . . . Question sir, with that record, why should we trust
   b you to run the nation's business?
   c TRUMP: Because I have used the laws of this country just like the
   d greatest people that you read about every day in business have used
       the laws of this country,
   e the chapter laws, to do a great job for my company, for myself, for
       my employees,
   f for my family, et cetera. I have never gone bankrupt, **by the way,**
   g **I** have never. But out of hundreds of deals –
   h WALLACE: No, but the concept sir –
   i TRUMP: Excuse me. Excuse me.

Trump's first use of "by the way" (1f) in the exchange with Wallace follows a statement about Trump's personal financial status (1c–f) in response to Wallace's question about Trump's trustworthiness following his past business deals involving bankruptcies (1a). Trump uses the DM "by the way" to shift away from his discussion of his exploitation of chapter laws, which could be perceived ambivalently by his audience, to tout his more positive personal financial status. It is important to note that this topic shift is embedded in the middle of his response, and is thus possibly obfuscated by the seemingly direct beginning of Trump's response in which he answers the moderator's "why" question (1a) with a straightforward turn-initial "because" (1c). In sum, the salient part of this answer – the beginning – stands in direct contrast to the typical candidate response beginning with no turn-initial "well," but Trump nonetheless shifts the direction of the debate discourse by exploiting another DM mid-response.

In this same exchange, Wallace follows up with a specific claim about job loss related to Trump's enterprise and debts regarding one particular bankruptcy filing, and Trump responds, again redirecting the discussion via "by the way" in a similar manner:

2    a   WALLACE: Well sir, let's just talk about the latest example. . . [applause]
    b  Which is Trump Entertainment Resorts, which went bankrupt in 2009. In that
    c  case alone, lenders to your company lost over $1 billion and more
    d  than 1,100 people were laid off.
    e  TRUMP: **Well**, I –
    f  WALLACE: Is that the way that you'd run the country?
    g  TRUMP: Let me just tell you about the lenders. First of all, those lenders aren't
    h  They are total babies killers. These are not the nice sweet little
    i  people that you think, **okay**? [laughter and applause] **You know, I mean** you're living in a
    j  world of the make-believe, Chris, you want to know the truth [applause].
    k  And I had the good sense to leave Atlantic City, which **by the way**, Caesars just went bankrupt.
    l  Every company, Chris can tell you, every company virtually in Atlantic City
    m  went bankrupt [laughter]. Every company. And let me just tell you.
    n  I had the good sense, and I've gotten a lot of credit in the financial pages,
    o  seven years ago I left Atlantic City before it totally cratered, and I made a lot of money in Atlantic City,
    p  and I'm very proud of it. I want to tell you that.
    q  Very, very proud of it.
    r  WALLACE: So –
    s  TRUMP: And **by the way**, this country right now owes $19 trillion.

t And they need somebody like me to straighten out that mess [applause].

In example (2), I have highlighted all DMs used by Trump throughout his response. In (2e), Trump attempts to respond to Wallace's claims about the bankruptcy of Trump Entertainment Resorts with an unusual turn-initial "Well" (2e), but gets cut off by the moderator, who proceeds to pose the challenging hypothetical question of whether Trump would run the country in the same manner (2f). Trump responds to this challenge by changing the topic to discuss the predatory nature of the lenders, without prefacing this evasion with a DM of any sort (2g). In (2i), Trump uses a double DM "you know, I mean" before accusing the moderator of "living in a world of the make-believe" (2i–j). This can be interpreted as a personal attack on the moderator, especially when one takes into account the ideologies associated with the practice of journalistic professionalism, which values sticking to facts, truth, and objectivity. The DMs used here, "you know" and "I mean," which have been offered a variety of interpretations by linguists, but have been attested to have a similarity in their basic meanings, with "you know" functioning to "invite addressee inferences" and "I mean" working to "forward upcoming adjustments" (Fox Tree & Schrock, 2002, p. 728, citing Jucker & Smith, 1998 and Schiffrin, 1987). In other words, these DMs work on the plane of participation framework by sending a message to the addressee (and in the debate context, to other nonaddressed hearers). On the plane of information state, they signal a shift in the speaker's footing. In this case, the DMs signal Trump's shift from attacking predatory lenders to attacking the moderator. The applause received after this attack (2j) indicates that the audience appreciates this shift.

In (2k), Trump again shifts the topic of discussion from his expression of pride regarding his decision to stop doing business in Atlantic City before the economy there totally collapsed, to providing timely examples supporting his claim: "by the way, Caesar's just went bankrupt" (2k–l). Here, the DM "by the way" shifts the focus of talk from his personal troubles in Atlantic City to refer to a large-scale issue with the entire industry. Trump then resumes to boast that his business benefited financially from the demise that others experienced (2o–q). When Wallace attempts to follow up on this statement in (2r), Trump interrupts to close this interchange, once again using "by the way" to preface the statement about the national debt: "this country right now owes $19 trillion" (2s). This last instance of "by the way" signals a complete topic shift, with the following proposition only bearing a remote topical connection to the previous discourse – i.e., discussion about debt and lenders. However, the problem of the US national debt has for years been a major talking point for presidential candidates, especially Republicans, and this particular statement allows Trump to end on a "high note" by saying that the country "needs someone like [him] to straighten out that mess" (2t). In sum, "by the way" allows Trump to fluidly shift the topic of his response away from propositions that could be damaging to his presidential self and toward topics that construct his identity as a candidate in tune with more important problems facing the nation.

### *"Believe me"*

Thus far, we have discussed elements of Trump's discursive style as it relates to turn-initial and turn-medial DMs in the debate data. The formal speeches examined in this study, which involve a different participation format, can nonetheless be analyzed for the presence and absence of similar features. Since a formal speech constitutes a single extended turn on the discourse plane of exchange structure, examining DMs in terms of their transition relevance place is not useful. However, political speeches can nonetheless be segmented into smaller turn-like units, which are punctuated by audience applause or other forms of interactional engagement (e.g., booing, laughing, chanting). In fact, politicians may use DMs or other familiar rhetorical units such as repetition (Fahnestock, 2011; Johnstone, 1996; Tannen, 2007) to signal discourse structure or invite audience interaction.

If we examine Trump's speeches for these units, we do find some patterns. One of these is the frequent use of the phrase "believe me," which is by now such a salient feature of Trump's idiolect that it has not only been discussed in the mainstream media as a feature of Trump's style, but also has been featured in various parodies and memes of the politician. The phrase was listed by a *Washington Post* reporter as one of the six "Trumpisms" to be expected in the early debates in August 2015 (Phillips, 2015), soon after Trump announced his candidacy. An entire *Boston Globe* article analyzing the phrase appeared in May 2016 (Viser, 2016). In this piece, Viser refers to "believe me" as a ubiquitous phrase that works to somehow discursively cancel out the ideological inconsistency and/or untruthfulness of Trump's discourse. He quotes a political science professor's take on the phrase, who likens it to the language of a used car salesman. A spokesperson for Trump also commented on his use of the expression, saying, "It's said from the heart with emphasis." Viser quantifies Trump's use of the expression in the debates – 30 times, compared to his opponents, who altogether used it three times, and the Democratic candidates, who never used it in the debates. Linguist George Lakoff provided an academic perspective in the piece from the perspective of cognitive linguistics, commenting on its function as an epistemic and evidential marker expressing the authoritativeness of the source; he is quoted as saying, "It assumes that knowledge comes from direct experience." Viser adds that the expression evokes Trump's other professional role in the sphere of business, and specifically the act of cutting business deals. He remarks that Trump appears to add it into written speeches, citing its ubiquity in his spoken address to AIPAC (13 times), compared to his written prepared remarks, in which it appeared only once.

Viser and the sources quoted in his article have pointed to several available social meanings associated with "believe me." These include an association with the speech act of negotiating a deal, the social type of a used car salesman, and as a discursive means to counter or cover up untrustworthiness. While these are all potentially at play in at least some interpretations of Trump's language, one element that this analysis of "believe me" has ignored is its role as a discourse marker or rhetorical strategy that indicates a turn ending and signals the possibility of, or potentially even invites verbal reaction from the audience.

This function is especially important to consider in his speeches, given that the monologic nature of a speech is quite distinct from the inherently dialogic nature of business negotiations and car dealing. Since the marker appeared so frequently in the AIPAC speech, let us examine a few examples of where and how it appears in this speech. The first use of "believe me" comes within the first few minutes of his speech following an introduction in which Trump recounts ways in which he has personally and financially supported Israel in the past. Trump then segues to the topic of his current speech in the following lines:

3   a TRUMP:   But I didn't come here tonight to pander to you about Israel.
   b   That's what politicians do.
   c   All talk, no action.
   d   **Believe me.**
   e AUDIENCE:      (Applause, 4 sec)
   f TRUMP:   I came here to speak to you about where I stand,
   g   on the future of American relations,
   h   with our strategic ally. . .

The next instance of the phrase comes just a couple minutes later, when he discusses the "disastrous deal with Iran":

4   a TRUMP:   I've studied this issue in *great* detail, I would say actually, *great*er by *far* than
    b   anybody else.
    c AUDIENCE:       (Laughter, 1 sec)
    d TRUMP:   ***Believe* me**. O:h **believe me** [audience laughter continues over Trump's talk].
    e AUDIENCE:       (Laughter, 2 sec) [Trump smiles wryly]
    f TRUMP:   And it's a *ba:d* deal.

In examples (3d) and (4d), "believe me" follows a point in the speech that does not relate to the overall purpose of the speech (i.e., to express a point of view related to America's relations with Israel and policy in the Middle East), but to metadiscursive quips about politics and politicians. In (3), Trump performs a common political speech act of identifying himself as a Washington outsider by telling his audience what he's *not*, doing oppositional identity work (Duranti, 2006; Sclafani, 2015, pp. 385–386) by distancing himself from the talk of politicians in an explicitly political speech. This statement, punctuated by "believe me", is followed by lengthy applause from the audience (3e).

Similarly, in (4), Trump makes a seemingly self-mocking quip through the use of self-aggrandizing comparatives, which cues audience laughter. Trump then continues, uttering the phrase "believe me" twice, with emphasis, while the audience continues to laugh. The elongated emphasizing DM "O:h" (4d) prefacing the repetition of the phrase seems to invite further laughter, at which point he pauses and smiles wryly, allowing the audience to continue (4e). In this sense, the phrase "believe me" functions at the level of participation framework as an invitation to involve the audience in some way in his evaluative nontopical remarks about political language and action. This is a marked move in a speech event that is traditionally monologic. This sets Trump up to provide the evaluative punchline to his statement and the resolution to this micronarrative he tells about studying the issues he is discussing. It may be argued that Trump's ability to create audience interaction in this setting work toward an indexical meaning that constructs him as a charismatic candidate.

The phrase "believe me" is not only uttered to punctuate metapolitical discursive moments in the speech, but it also serves to punctuate substantive points of his topical argument. In the next example, Trump is describing the second point of his plan regarding relations with Iran:

5   a TRUMP:     Iran is the *bigg*est *spon*sor of terrorism around the world,
    b       And we will *work* to dis*man*tle that reach.
    c   **Be*lieve* me. Be*lieve* me.**
    d AUDIENCE:       (Applause, 5 sec)
    e TRUMP:     Third at the very least. . .

It is important to notice that again in this example, the phrase is repeated and emphasized, and invites extensive applause from the audience. While Viser and Phillips's analyses are right to point out that Trump uses this expression extensively, and markedly more than other candidates, what the quantitative focus on "believe me" in their analyses does not capture is how it works to create audience involvement in his speech – a central function that distinguishes spoken from written discourse (Chafe, 1985; Tannen, 1982) and has been described as a definitional feature of conversation (Gumperz, 1982; Tannen, 2007). As Tannen (2007) has outlined, conversational involvement strategies include both sound- and sense-based features. Sound-based strategies include repetition of various segments, from phonological to discursive, and meaning-based strategies include figures of speech such as indirectness, ellipses, tropes, dialogue, imagery, and narrative. Trump's repetitive and emphatic "believe me" clearly works as an involvement strategy at the level of both sound and meaning. Additionally, through its imperative syntactic form and its role as a first pair part of an adjacency pair (Schegloff & Sacks, 1973), it could be argued that the phrase commands the audience into a particular cognitive state, such as a state of belief in the speaker. The use of this phrase is also a clear example of what Fairclough (1992; see also Talbot, 1995) refers to as "synthetic personalization" – a phenomenon in which the language of mass media communication is tailored in such a way that targets an implied hearer or reader, rendering the illusion of the speaker having an intimate conversation with an individual in the audience.

## *Epistrophic punctuation*

Trump's stock phrase "believe me" might be considered one example of a larger pattern in his rhetoric, which I refer to as **epistrophic punctuation**, or the repetition of short phrases, often ones that convey an affective or epistemic stance, that appear at the end of rhetorical units in his speeches. The examples of "believe me" examined earlier (3–5) are each examples of this phenomenon, occurring in places where he is ending a cohesive rhetorical unit within his speech, but Trump uses other forms of epistrophic punctuation in the same manner. Let us examine the following excerpt, again from the AIPAC speech, in which Trump is still discussing the situation in Iran:

6   a TRUMP:   . . . The deal is silent on test missiles.
    b      But those tests do violate the United Nations Security council resolutions.
    c      The problem is no one has done anything about it.
    d      **We will, we will.** I promise, **we will.**
    e AUDIENCE:        (Cheers, applause.)
    f TRUMP:   Thank you. Which brings me to my next point. . .

Similar to the placement and function of "believe me" in (5), which precedes an explicit mention that he is proceeding to talk about another point via the listing device "third" (5e), the repetitive use of "we will" in example (6d) invites the audience's participation, for which Trump expresses thanks before telling the audience that he is moving on to his next point. In the following excerpt from the AIPAC speech, Trump similarly repeats a full clause "we [wi]ll get it solved" to wrap up a point before changing the topic:

7   a TRUMP:   President Obama thinks that applying pressure to Israel will force the issue.
    b      But it's precisely the opposite that happens.
    c      Already half of the population Palestine has been taken over by the
    d      Palestinian ISIS and Hamas, and the other half refuses to confront the first half,
    e      so it's a very difficult situation that's never going to get solved unless you have
    f      great leadership right here in the United States.
    g      **We'll get it solved.** One way or the other, **we will get it solved.**
    f      (Applause)
    g      But when the United States stands with Israel,
    f      the chances of peace really rise and rises exponentially.
    g      That's what will happen when Donald Trump is president of the United States.

In excerpt (7), Trump shifts from talking about the current poor state of relations between the United States and the Middle East as a result of President Obama's policies (7a–d), referring to the situation as "a very difficult situation that's never going to get solved" (7d–e). At this point, Trump introduces a possible exception to this undesirable outcome: "Unless you have great leadership right here in the US" (7e–f). In (7g), he proposes himself, in conjunction with his audience, using the inclusive pronoun "we," as a solution to this problem and as an agent to fill the absence of "great leadership." Epistrophic punctuation – the repetition of "we [wi]ll get it solved" in (7g) – allows him again to end on a positive note and this time an inclusive note with the use of the plural pronoun, in contrast to singular "believe me." This pattern of employing epistrophic punctuation to conclude a speech segment on a "high note" parallels Trump's style of debate response analyzed in (2). We can see by analyzing the politician's speech patterns and use of DMs and repetition in both debate and speech contexts that these discourse strategies work in consort with patterns in the overall arc of Trump's larger discourse units. They also allow him to shift both the topic and his tone throughout his speech, while cuing his audience into these shifts in sometimes subtle ways, at the same time as he involves them into his talk in contexts that don't normally invite audience participation.

## Conclusion

In summary, this chapter has investigated several discourse marking strategies related to Donald Trump's idiosyncratic style of public speaking in debate and formal speech contexts. Some of these features have received attention in the mainstream media, such as his tendency to utter "believe me," while others, like his relative lack of turn-initial "well," have gone under the radar of journalistic analyses of his rhetorical style.

Specifically, I demonstrated that Trump's use of DMs, and specifically his relatively infrequent reliance on the use of turn-initial "well" as a topic-refocusing device, work toward the construction of his identity as a strong and straightforward debater because he appears to answer questions in a direct manner by not presenting his positions with DMs indicating qualification or evasion. On the other hand, Trump uses the phrase "by the way" more frequently than other candidates (and exclusively in debates examined here) as a way to accomplish the same sorts of evasions that "well" has been characterized as indicating in past research. Because "by the way" occurs turn-medially, it does not cue a "dodge" at the outset and also functions as a power move, showing that the candidate can assert epistemic status over his opponents as well as the moderator by proposing new topics that hadn't been previously introduced in the debate. Donald Trump's frequent use of "believe me", on the other hand, was shown to play an important role in structuring his talk and encouraging audience participation in the context of monologic speeches.

With a solid understanding of these features as they work in the construction of a particular presidential identity for Donald Trump, we now turn to examine some of the interactional discourse strategies that Trump employs in debates and speeches, and how they work in the construction of his political brand and presidential persona. The next chapter will deal with interruption, constructed dialogue and other forms of double-voicing, along with Trump's idiosyncratic use of co-speech gesture.

## Note

1   While I do not conduct a detailed analysis of stylistic variation between the scripted and unscripted speeches here, this is certainly an area that merits further attention in future research.

# 3 Trump's idiolect
## Interactional devices

## Introduction

In the previous chapter, I discussed linguistic features of Donald Trump's idiosyncratic style that set him apart from the other candidates in the 2016 GOP primaries and in recent Republican presidential electoral history in general. I focused specifically on discourse-marking devices, including the discourse markers "well" and "by the way," and discussed how they operated in managing evasions in the context of answering questions during debates. Trump's habit of employing "believe me" as a discourse marker was also shown to function as a building block in his presidential identity construction, and it functioned along with other types of epistrophic punctuation as a device to invite audience involvement in speech-giving contexts. While Chapter 2 focused on features that help scaffold the structure of his discourse, I now turn to the patterned use of particular interactional devices in Donald Trump's speech and examine how these operate on multiple levels of discourse structure. I also consider how they serve as contextualization cues that allow the audience to interpret the language of Donald Trump as emanating from a particular brand of presidential persona. Specifically, I address the use of Trump's use of interruption in debates, his use of constructed dialogue and other types of double-voiced discourse in both speeches and debates, and his use of idiosyncratic co-speech gestures, which work together to consolidate Trump's style and presidential identity.

## Interruption as a means of power and control

Interruption as an element of style is one of the most commonly studied features of conversational interaction. Conversation analysts have been studying the mechanics of overlapping speech since the 1970s (e.g., Sacks, Schegloff, & Jefferson, 1974). Tannen (1990) differentiates between mechanical overlap, or the presence of two voices at once, and interruption, which involves the interpretation that one's speaking rights have been violated. Interruption, whether through overlap, topic shifting, or other means, has been described by linguists as one way to gain and maintain control of the conversational floor (e.g., Zimmerman & West, 1975).

Tannen (1993), however, clarifies that what many consider to be interruptive behavior is polysemous and ambiguous: it can be seen as either a power or connection maneuver. In her work on New York Jewish conversational style, for example, Tannen (1981) demonstrates that when New Yorkers talk to each other, conversational overlap is employed in a positive way to show involvement in conversation and is interpreted as such by interlocutors of the same background. However, when the same involvement strategy is used with a speaker from California who doesn't share the same norms for displaying involvement and considerateness in conversation, the same linguistic maneuver is viewed as an attempt to dominate the conversation.

When we move from the context of everyday sociable conversation to the institutional context of political interviews and debates, which have specific participation formats, participant roles and their institutionally determined power relationships, overlapping speech, and other potentially interruptive strategies may take on specific social meanings. In American presidential debates, moderators are accorded the most powerful roles in their ability to direct the speech event in terms of the selection of topic, speaker, and length of turn. In presidential primary debates, where there are often several (and in the 2015–2016 debates, up to a dozen) candidates who wish to gain the floor to respond to a moderator's question and put forth their own particular presidential self, there are actually quite a few opportunities for back and forth discussion and "jumping in" to the debate, as the moderators tend to control the conversational floor for all but a few minutes of the entire event.

In analyzing Trump's speech patterns in the interactional contexts of the debates and interviews, certain patterns emerge in terms of his interruptive style that are quite unlike his primary opponents and that play a role in distinguishing his style and contribute to his identity construction as a powerful, decisive, outsider candidate. In the three debates analyzed in detail in this study, Trump overlaps and interjects comments into the moderator's questions to a much greater extent than other candidates. This pattern became even more apparent in the general debates, during which Trump received a great deal of attention in the media for his constant interruption of Hillary Clinton and the debate moderators. While the general debates won't be discussed here, parodies of them and his interrupting style will be discussed in Chapter 4.

Before providing examples of Trump's interruptions in the primary debates, it will be useful to briefly discuss the general template of moderator questions in these debates. As alluded to earlier in the discussion of discourse marking, questions posed to candidates are rarely single-proposition questions, but contain discursively complex setups that provide background information on (1) what the candidate being questioned has said or done in the past, (2) what another candidate has said or done, or (3) a current state of affairs or actions of the incumbent. As such, a moderator's question often takes the form of multiple declarative clauses prefacing an interrogative. The following is one typical example of such a question, which comes from the Fox News moderator Chris Wallace in the August 6, 2015, debate in Cleveland:

8    a  WALLACE:  Governor Christie, I want to engage you and Governor Huckabee in a subject
     b  that is a big issue in both of your campaigns, and that is entitlement reform.
     c  You say that you – to save the system that you want to raise the retirement age –
     d  have to raise the retirement age, and to cut benefits for Social Security and Medicare,
     e  and you say that some of the candidates here on this stage are lying.
     f  Governor Huckabee says he can save Social Security and Medicare without doing any of that.
     g  Is he lying?"

In this fairly typical example, the moderator's question first contains a vocative singling out the candidate to whom the question is being asked, but also involves reference to a third party (another candidate on stage) and an announcement of the topical issue (8a–b). Next, the moderator reports the past speech of the candidate (8b–e), comparing it to a statement made by the third party on the same topic (8f–g). Finally, he asks the candidate to evaluate the statement made by the third party with the interrogative, "Is he lying?" (8g).

As I have discussed elsewhere (Sclafani, 2014), complex questions such as this one are the norm in presidential debates, and, usually, the moderator manages to complete reading the entire prepared question before a candidate begins to respond. However, in examining the debates in which Donald Trump participated, he is found on several occasions to interrupt the moderator's questioning sequence with a fairly predictable type of interjection.

For example, in the August 6, 2015, debate in Cleveland, Trump interjects Fox News moderator Megyn Kelly's questions multiple times:

9  a KELLY:    Mr. Trump, one of the things people love about you is you speak your mind and

   b    you don't use a politician's filter. However, that is not without its downsides, in

   c    particular, when it comes to women. You've called women you don't like

   d    "fat pigs, [laughter] dogs, slobs, and disgusting animals." Your Twitter account –

   e TRUMP:    [Shaking finger] Only Rosie O'Donnell [audience laughter, applause].

   f KELLY:    No, it wasn't. [Applause] Your Twitter account – [applause/cheers 15 secs]

   g TRUMP:    Thank you.

   h KELLY:    For the record, it was well beyond Rosie O'Donnell.

   i TRUMP:    Yes, I'm sure it was.

   j KELLY:    Your Twitter account has several disparaging comments about women's looks.

   k    You once told a contestant on *Celebrity Apprentice* it would be a pretty picture to see her on her knees.

   l    Does that sound to you like the temperament of a man

   m    we should elect as president, and how will you answer the charge from Hillary Clinton,

   n    who was likely to be the Democratic nominee,

   o    that you are part of the war on women?

   p TRUMP:    I think the big problem this country has is being politically correct. I've been ch –

   q    [Applause] . . . .

This moment was one of the most frequently replayed excerpts from the early primary debates, the reason for which is clear: the interaction between Kelly and Trump is highly confrontational but also very humorous to the audience, both due to Kelly's direct quotation of the candidate's past remarks about women (9c–d, j–k) and Trump's qualification of Kelly's claim (9e) and subsequent admission to the extent of his past insults (9i). In this exchange, Trump interrupts Kelly mid-question twice (8e, g) and then responds to her correction that he insulted women other than Rosie O'Donnell (9i).

Candidate interruptions in debate contexts in general can be considered face threatening to the candidate's positive face, as they construct an image of the candidate as willfully ignoring the established turn-taking norms of the speech event. When they interrupt a moderator's question in particular, candidates may be viewed as challenging the institutionally endowed power of the moderator and attempting to control the exchange and participation format to their advantage. Such behavior may be perceived as "unpresidential" by viewers and voters, who esteem qualities like "fairness" and "diplomacy" as ideal characteristics of a president. However, the way in which Trump manages his interruptive behavior in this interaction appeals on another level – by creating solidarity with the audience through the use of a lighthearted, jocular demeanor. He is clearly successful in using this strategy within the debate hall, as he receives extensive applause and cheers from the audience (9f).

While it is impossible to uncover whether the audience is applauding the content of his past insults, the targets of his insults, or the way he manages the interaction, the fact that he received 15 seconds of straight applause and cheers in a debate where it was explicitly announced at the outset that only moderate audience reaction would be acceptable makes it clear that this interaction was enjoyed on some level by the viewing public. It also received a great deal of attention in the press following the debate and commenced a months-long feud between Trump and Kelly (Chavez, Stracqualursi, & Keneally, 2016). Trump's unapologetic and (for many viewers) humorous style of interruption continued throughout the primaries and the general election, and worked to his advantage because they allowed him to gain access to the debate floor with infrequent vocal opposition from his opponents or the moderator. Hall, Goldstein, and Ingram (2016), in their analysis of Trump's use of gesture and its entertainment value, succinctly sum up this phenomenon of audience appreciation of Trump's insulting style and his overall carnivalesque behavior in public appearances: "It is hard to critique a clown: we are too busy laughing" (3). I will return to this argument later in the chapter when I summarize in more detail Hall et al.'s analysis of gesture as an element of Trump's idiomatic style. However, it is important to note that in his construction of a presidential self, Trump relies on his already well-known persona from his earlier roles as a combative, no-holds-barred, cutthroat executive on his reality television show; this established brand gives him an advantage over the other candidates because he can recruit his prepolitical brand for new communicative purposes. Another potential reason that the public appreciates his aggressive behavior in debates and other public appearances is because, quite simply, they recognize it, and it thus works to strengthen his political brand and differentiate him among a dozen candidates vying for the nomination.

## Constructed dialogue in a monologic context

Another feature of Trump's discursive style worth examining is his use of direct reported speech in both monologic (speeches) and dialogic (debates) contexts. The use of direct reported speech, or constructed dialogue, as Tannen (2007) has termed it, is an intertextual strategy that has been showed to play an important role in both involvement and persuasion in spoken conversational discourse. The term "constructed" emphasizes the change in meaning that necessarily accompanies the importation of a prior text (Becker, 2000) into a new speaking context. It also, as Tannen demonstrates, highlights the fact that speech is oftentimes not strictly reported – for example, in cases where one uses direct reports to summarize a whole conversation, when one voices one's own or another's thoughts rather than words, or when a nonhuman speaker (e.g., a family pet, a stuffed animal) is voiced.

A few studies have highlighted the importance of constructed dialogue in political discourse. Gordon (2004), for example, demonstrates how a family uses constructed dialogue – in this case, recycling quotations of a presidential candidate – in order to negatively evaluate the candidate and construct a coherent political family identity as supporters of the opposing political party. Kuo (2001) demonstrates that constructed dialogue plays a role in self-promotion and other-denigration in debate contexts, arguing that the act of articulating someone else's words works to objectify praise of oneself and vilification of one's opponents. Kuo also points out that direct quotation can work as a strategy to downplay epistemic status by distancing oneself from the source of one's knowledge. In this sense, the use of direct quotation can protect the speaker from charges of lying or misrepresenting the truth (see also Wortham & Locher, 1999). Finally, Kuo points out that the relative amount of direct reported speech in candidates' debate performances also contributes to stylistic differences, showing that debaters with more "casual" styles use more constructed dialogue than those with more formal styles. Looking at variation in the use of direct versus indirect reported speech and the sources of the reports in journalistic and online discourse, my earlier research (Sclafani, 2008b, 2009) has also found that this strategy plays a role in highlighting certain voices while suppressing others, thus constructing and reaffirming relations of power between represented individuals.

In both his monologic speeches and in dialogic interviews and debate contexts, Donald Trump makes extensive use of constructed dialogue in a variety of ways that relate to the various aforementioned functions of the discourse strategy. Let us first consider Mr. Trump's use of constructed dialogue in a monologic context, taking his candidacy announcement speech as an example. In this speech, there are several instances of constructed dialogue in which the candidate animates both himself and others in conversation. These others include concerned voters, his audience (via second-person "you"), his family, members of the media, Republican candidates, and representatives of institutions like "the big banks." Through constructed dialogue, Donald Trump positions himself as a financially independent, strong, ambitious, outsider candidate who is ready to respond to the problems of the common American.

In the following excerpt from this speech, Trump voices his family's concern over his decision to run for president:

10  a TRUMP:   We need – we need somebody –
   b   we need somebody that literally will take this country and make it great again.
   c   We can do that.
   d   And I will tell you, I love my life.
   e   I have a wonderful family.
   f   They're saying, "Dad, you're going to do something that's going to be so tough."
   g   You know, all of my life, I've heard that a truly successful person,
   h   a really, really successful person and even modestly successful
   i   cannot run for public office. Just can't happen.
   j   And yet that's the kind of mindset that you need to make this country great again.
   k   So ladies and gentlemen. . .
   l   I am officially running  . . . for president of the United States,
   m   and we are going to make our country great again.

In this excerpt, Trump directly voices the admonition of his family members (and more specifically, his children, via the kinship-referring term "Dad") about how "tough" it is to run for president (10f). He then indirectly voices another unspecified principal (when he says "all my life, I've heard . . .") who posits that successful people "cannot" run for office (10g–i). These voices – the directly voiced familial relations and indirectly voiced others – come together in his speech to construct a chorus of opposition to his decision to run for office, directly setting up his official announcement of candidacy as a conscious decision to take on this task, despite its impracticality for someone in his position, for the greater good of the nation. As such, the use of direct constructed dialogue in consort with unspecified other voices works to construct a presidential self as someone who is not only strong but also willing to make a sacrifice for the nation. By saying that "even modestly successful people cannot run" (10h), he also denigrates career politicians by implying that other past and current candidates have tended to be relatively unsuccessful (presumably in comparison to himself), which in turn reinforces his own position as a political outsider. This is a personal identity that resurfaces quite frequently in other forms throughout his campaign, most often through his previously discussed statement that career politicians are "all talk, no action."

Another use of constructed dialogue in Donald Trump's candidacy speech is to introduce his position on international trade by illustrating the problems of American manufacturers. In the following excerpt, Trump recounts an interaction he had with one such friend, voicing both sides of the conversation via constructed dialogue:

11  a TRUMP:   A friend of mine who's a great manufacturer, calls me up
       a few weeks ago.
    b   He's very upset. I said, "What's your problem?"
    c   He said, "You know, I make great product."
    d   And I said, "I know. I know that because I buy the product."
    e   He said, "I can't get it into China. They won't accept it.
    f   I sent a boat over and they actually sent it back.
    g   They talked about environmental,
    h   they talked about all sorts of crap that had nothing to do with it."
    i   I said, "Oh, wait a minute, that's terrible. Does anyone know this?"
    j   He said, "Yeah, they do it all the time with other people."
    k   I said, "They send it back?"
    l   "Yeah. So I finally got it over there and they charged me a big
       tariff.
    m   They're not supposed to be doing that. I told them."

Following this recounted conversation with the manufacturer, Trump begins describing the current trade situation with China, giving specific examples of companies that have dealt with it (such as the aerospace corporation Boeing), and using a sports metaphor to illustrate the power imbalance the United States faces in trade with China. In the conversation he recounts with the manufacturer in (11), Trump positions himself as having epistemic authority and firsthand awareness of the "greatness" of his friend's product since he is a consumer of it, but as having been unaware of the problem relating to exporting it. In this conversation, Trump learns through this conversation with his friend that the problem is not isolated but a systemic issue regarding trade policy and one that is not fair. Trump uses this story to launch into an explanation of how he has dealt with China personally and how the cards are stacked against the United States in matters of international trade. While the candidate does not specify what these laws are, or how they are unfair, or how they might be remedied, he introduces his audience to the problem by voicing how he *personally* became aware of the problem – as a consumer, in a personal conversation with a friend who produces his product.

In this way, Trump manages to construct what I have previously referred to as "existential coherence" (Duranti, 2006) in his candidacy by constructing his present position as a presidential candidate as a natural extension of the past. That is, he first learned of trade problems faced by American manufacturers in his position as a consumer and as a member of a community of business entrepreneurs, and then faced them himself as a businessman, both of which have led to his current position as a presidential candidate with sufficient intimate knowledge about trade problems to know how it should be remedied. In fact, Trump continues this speech by animating an extended hypothetical conversation between himself and the president of Ford Motor Company to illustrate how he would solve the problem of manufacturing jobs being moved abroad, using constructed dialogue with various others to take the audience from his first identification of a problem to his future solution in his role as president.

This type of narrative of experience and self-positioning as a political outsider is not unique to the discourse of Donald Trump and is one that has been observed in the discourse of other political candidates (see e.g., Duranti, 2006; Sclafani, 2015), but it is one that is voiced explicitly through constructed dialogue in this speech and in a context that serves as an introduction to the candidate's position on foreign trade. In this sense, constructed dialogue functions in ways that have been described as characteristic of conversational discourse (Gordon, 2004; Tannen, 2007) – as a way of constructing alignments, creating involvement, and also ways that have been attested in the rhetoric of political debates (Kuo, 2001), serving the function of positive self-promotion and other-denigration. Trump's use of this discourse strategy might be considered an example of what political analysts have described as the highly conversational nature of Donald Trump's style and seems to substantiate his frequently attested ability to "connect" with voters.

Other instances of constructed dialogue in Trump's announcement speech come in the form of quoting members of the media and their reactions to him. Considering that Trump's vocalization about issues with media bias received substantial airtime throughout his general election campaign (and continue to do so during his presidency), it is worth considering his early articulations of problematic interactions with the media here. In the following excerpt, Trump transitions from his discussion about Ford and trade deals to talk about his temperament and qualities that he believes are important for a presidential candidate to have in this election cycle. He introduces this topic by mentioning that he's been told he is "not a nice person" by members of the media, admitting first that it's true and then expressing his own opposing opinion of himself and the views of his family members:

12   a TRUMP:   Somebody said to me the other day, a reporter, a very nice
                reporter,
     b          "But, Mr. Trump, you're not a nice person."
     c          That's true. But actually I am. I think I am a nice person.
     d          People that know me, like me.
     e          Does my family like me? I think so, right. Look at my family.

This excerpt may sound self-contradictory in the sense that Trump ratifies the view of the "very nice reporter" that he is "not a nice person" just before stating that he believes he in fact is nice; it has largely been excerpts like this that have been taken from Trump's speeches and described as "incoherent" in the mainstream media. However, it can be argued that this apparent contradiction appeals to an interpretation of Trump's existential coherence at another level. At this early point in his campaign, Donald Trump was widely known for his long-term reality television role on *The Apprentice*, playing a boss who was notably "not nice." Here, he seems to be contrasting his public persona with his persona in the private sphere of his family in which he believes he is considered "nice." This transition from his public to private self in this excerpt serves as a preface for him to introduce his family members to the audience, which is an important element of a presidential campaign announcement, considering both the symbolic importance of the first family in the American political sphere (Mayo, 2000) and the social capital that talk about family can provide a parent, and especially a man, in the context of constructing a professional leadership identity (Gordon, Tannen, & Sacknovitz, 2007; Kendall, 2006).

Following some talk in which he praises specific family members, Trump reanimates the conversation he had with the reporter, revoicing the same question and his response more elaborately:

13   a TRUMP:   So the reporter said to me the other day,
     b          "But, Mr. Trump, you're not a nice person. How can you get peo-
                ple to vote for you?"

c  I said, "I don't know."
d  I said, "I think that number one, I am a nice person.
e  I give a lot of money away to charities and other things.
f  I think I'm actually a very nice person."
g  But, I said, "This is going to be an election that's based on competence,
h  because people are tired of these nice people.

This time, when Trump constructs the voice of the reporter stating that he is not a nice person, it is followed by a logical question – "How can you get people to vote for you?" – that is presumably based on the following syllogism:

- Successful presidential candidates are always nice. (Major premise)
- You are not nice. (Minor premise)
- You will not be a successful candidate. (Conclusion)

In the response that Trump constructs as having given the reporter, he again contradicts the minor premise that was explicitly stated by the reporter and continues to question the unstated major premise on which the question was based – that a good presidential candidate is a "nice" candidate. As was discussed in Chapter 1, the rise of Donald Trump in the 2016 Republican primaries may be an indication that what Robin Lakoff's described as the rise of Niceness in American politics may now be in question, and in this moment, Trump explicitly questions the status quo of Niceness himself.

It is important to note that in his response, there is another implicit assumption – that a candidate cannot be both nice and competent at once. This assumption does not get explicitly voiced, nor does it get questioned by the reporter within the constructed dialogue. In this way, Donald Trump manages to bring to the surface the often unstated premises of logical arguments against his candidacy but leaves his own premises left unstated. This pattern, which emerges here in constructed dialogue in his candidacy announcement, continues throughout his primary campaign and into the general election, branding the candidate as the Nasty response to (what he sees as) decades of Nice-But-Ineffective leaders.

Throughout the remainder of his nomination speech, Trump voices several other characters with whom he has had conversations, and a similar pattern ensues. Through these conversations, he represents how he can help common Americans, including the manufacturer described earlier, as well as a woman who wants to buy guns to protect herself. He uses other public figures, like the reporter in (13) and elsewhere; he voices "the pundits" to voice opposition to his candidacy in the mainstream media, which is a voice that grows much louder throughout his campaign, as a basis for preempting and responding to doubts regarding the viability of his presidential brand. And Trump voices people in powerful positions, like the president of Ford or "one of the big banks" or the "establishment" GOP candidates, in ways that place them in subordinate positions to himself by performing speech acts that implicate their deferent positions (e.g., imploring him for financial support or complying with his demands).

## Constructed dialogue in a dialogic context

Thus far, I have only considered Trump's use of constructed dialogue in a monologic context, but as other scholars have noted (Kuo, 2001; Lauerbach, 2006), constructed dialogue plays an important role in dialogic political discourse contexts like debates and interviews as well. Interestingly, when the use of constructed dialogue by Trump in the debates is compared to the examples just described in the monologic context of his candidacy announcement speech, a different pattern emerges. In the debate context, Trump does construct voices of others in his talk, but rather than revoicing personal interactions that contain a two-way dialogue, his direct reports of speech – including both self- and other-quotation – are one-way interactions. An additional difference that surfaces is the types of others whose voices are constructed by Trump. Whereas in his announcement speech, the individual referred to could be identified by the audience, whether in terms of biographical or categorical identification (Schiffrin, 1977; Schegloff, 1968), the people whose voices Trump animates in the debate tend to be more vaguely referenced. Both types of constructed dialogue – self-reports and vague other-reports – tend to perform the same function of amplifying Trump's own voice and the position he is taking in the interactional context of the debate.

First, let us examine instances in which Trump voices his own past speech in the debates. Extract (14) comes from the August 6 debate in Cleveland and illustrates Trump's response to moderator Chris Wallace's request for Trump to share proof regarding his allegations that the Mexican government is sending criminals across the border:

14  a TRUMP:   So, if it weren't for me,
    b     you wouldn't even be talking about illegal immigration, Chris.
    c     You wouldn't even be talking about it [applause].
    d     This was not a subject that was on anybody's mind until I brought it up at my announcement
    e     and I said, "Mexico is sending."
    f     Except the reporters, because they're a very dishonest lot,

g generally speaking in the world of politics, they didn't cover my statement the

h way I said it.

Similarly, in extract (15), from the February 6, 2016, debate in New Hampshire, Trump responds to a question by ABC moderator David Muir requesting that he respond to an attack by his primary opponent Senator Ted Cruz regarding his temperament. After contesting Cruz's accusation that Trump would be likely to "nuke Denmark," Trump posits that he has "the best temperament" and illustrates his political savvy by stating that he was the first to talk about the nation's "problem" with Muslims:

15 a TRUMP:  Nobody else wanted to mention the problem.

   b I brought it up. I took a lot of heat. . .

   c And remember this, I'm the only one up here, when the war in Iraq –

   d In Iraq, I was the one that said,

   e "Don't go, don't do it, you're going to destabilize the Middle East."

Again, in the March 10 debate, Trump uses constructed dialogue in the form of self-quotation in response to Ted Cruz's statement of his position against the Iran deal, which Cruz contrasts with Trump's position:

16 a TRUMP:  I was against the giving of the money at all cost.

   b I said, "Don't negotiate at all until you get the prisoners back.

   c If the prisoners don't come back early" – three years ago.

   d One of the longest negotiations I've ever seen, by the way. . .

In debate extracts (14)–(16), which are representative of the type of self-quotation performed by Trump throughout the primary debates, he uses constructed dialogue to report what he has said on previous occasions. In (14) and (15), he prefaces what he has said with references to the idea that others were *not* talking about this specific topic, with the implication that in making these statements on prior occasions, *he* was agentive in bringing up important issues that matter to the public. In the context of a primary debate, one can see this as a direct challenge to the moderator, whose job is to formulate questions for the candidates on topics that are deemed important by voters. In (16), Trump uses constructed dialogue to voice his previous position on a policy that contradicts another candidate's characterization of his position, thus directly challenging his opponent. In these examples, the use of constructed dialogue serves as a megaphone, amplifying the current position Trump presents in the debates by voicing his current stance as a repetition of what he's said before. In this sense, self-quotation serves to construct a presidential image that is consistent over time as a candidate of "conviction" who does not change his mind according to the political winds. This self-presentation contrasts with a well-known type of particular political character that is negatively evaluated – that of the flip-flopper (Lempert, 2011; Lempert & Silverstein, 2012). Additionally, Trump's constructions of his own past utterance serve to position him as a luminary type of candidate in the face of both his opponents and the media in the sense that he was the only one with the vision that these topics needed to be discussed at an earlier point in time.

At the same time, it might be considered that Trump does some identity repair work through constructed dialogue in (14), because his revoicing of what he said is constructed elliptically – "Mexico is sending (X)" – leaving out the important objects ("criminals, rapists, drug dealers") referred to in the moderator's question, a statement for which Trump earned a major backlash in the media and accusations of blatant xenophobia following his announcement speech. This example makes particularly apparent the critical power of intertextual devices in the way that they both amplify and suppress certain voices.

If we move away from self-quotation to examine the way in which Trump voices various others in the debates, we also find indicative patterns that relate to his overall construction of a presidential identity. It should be noted that there are many more occasions in which Trump makes reference to what others say *without* directly reporting speech in the debates than when he *does* animate others' voices. An example of this emerged in previous examples in which he contrasted his own past words with what others *weren't* talking about (15). We see these vague references to others' speech elsewhere in the debates, as the following excerpts illustrate. In (17), Trump continues to defend his statement regarding illegal immigration from Mexico in response to the moderator's pressure for evidence that was described in (14):

17 a TRUMP: Border patrol, people I deal with, that I talk to,
   b       they say this is what's happening.

Similarly, in the February debate in New Hampshire, Trump responds to questions about his position on military intervention in North Korea by talking about his knowledge of China's relationship with the country based on his previous business dealings in the country:

18 a TRUMP: I deal with [the Chinese]. They tell me.
   b       They have total, absolute control, practically, of North Korea.

In (17) and (18), Trump makes references to "they" – "people that I deal with, that I talk to" – who "tell" and "say" to him what is happening, without specifying who these sources are and, furthermore, without attributing any direct speech to them that provides insight into what exactly has been said. The effect here is that in responding to questions about foreign relations in the debate, an area that Trump was known to be less versed in given his background as a political outsider, Trump manages to convey some sense of authority by using markers of evidentiality that allude to direct and intimate experience with people who know about these issues. He capitalizes on his background as a businessman to place himself in interaction with people who work at the US-Mexico border and in interaction with the Chinese, who hold a strategic position between the United States and North Korea, in order to construct epistemic authority even if his responses are lacking in terms of content and the pronouncement of an actual position related to international policy. This is not unlike findings from previous research (Sclafani, 2015) showing that candidates use references to others, and specifically family members in the armed forces, to illustrate their knowledge and understanding of matters related to national security.

When Trump *does* directly voice others in debates, his reference to others takes a similarly vague form. For example, in (18), Trump responds to a question about eminent domain during the New Hampshire debate:

19  a TRUMP:   And what a lot of people don't know because they were all saying,
    b          "Oh, you're going to take their property."
    c          When eminent domain is used on somebody's property they get a fortune.

And in (20), Trump responds to a question about his call for a pause on green cards issued to foreign workers by reporting his Disney endorsement during the March debate in Florida:

20  a TRUMP:   Very importantly, the Disney workers endorsed me, as you probably read.
    b          And I got a full endorsement because they are the ones that said,
    c          And they had a news conference, and they said,
    d          "He's the only one that's going to be able to fix it. Because it is a mess."

In these examples, Trump voices various others. In (19) the exact referents are not clear in either biographical or categorical terms – "a lot of people."

In (20), the referent to which the direct reported speech can be attributed is the Disney workers' union members. However, it should be noted in both cases that Trump refers to *collectives* rather than individuals, and the speech emanating from these collectives serves a similar function to the self-quotations analyzed previously: they amplify the current speaker's voice by providing either additional support for the positions he expresses in the debate (via an official endorsement in (20)), or by animating the opposing voice against which Trump is arguing (in (19)). While the use of constructed dialogue in debate contexts is not unique to the rhetoric of Donald Trump, his tendency to voice *ambiguous collective others* through both direct and indirect reports of speech are particular to his style and arguably work in the discursive construction of his populist message.

In sum, this analysis of the use of constructed dialogue in monologic and dialogic contexts illustrates that Donald Trump uses this strategy for various purposes in different types of speech events. In his candidacy announcement speech, he uses constructed dialogue to connect with his audience by recounting narratives of interactions he's had with his family, with concerned citizens, and with the media. Through these interactions, he positions himself as a strong, independent, competent, outsider candidate, who may not be the "nicest" candidate in the field but who is willing to put aside his successful career in business for the good of the nation and is the most prepared to get the job of president done. In the debates, by contrast, Trump uses direct and indirect quotation for persuasive purposes in order to build epistemic authority on issues related to international relations, illustrate his existential coherence in a larger narrative of how he transitioned from the sphere of business to that of politics, and, importantly, as a megaphone to amplify his own voice through repetition of his past words and echo his position through the voices of others.

## Co-speech gesture in interaction

One of the major features of Donald Trump's communicative style that has been the subject of ample attention in the media and has been highlighted in parodies of the candidate is his idiosyncratic use of gesture and facial expressions in public speaking events. The most commonly remarked upon features are his resting "scowl" face, affected smirks, and hand gestures. The latter has been commented on frequently both in terms of the broad repertoire that his manual gestures encompass and by the gestural space they span, occupying a notably larger space than the gestures of other politicians.

Because this chapter has focused on linguistic elements of Trump's style, I do not perform an exhaustive analysis of his gesture here, but it is an important element of his style to at least mention before moving on to talk about impressions and parodies of the candidate, since this stylistic device does feature into various types of metadiscourse on Donald Trump's discursive style. Instead of performing a novel analysis of co-speech gesture, I summarize an in-depth analysis of his gesture conducted by Hall, Goldstein, and Ingram (2016), and provide additional commentary on how his gestures articulate with linguistic features analyzed here, and how they cluster with linguistic aspects of Trump's style and coalesce in the construction of a particular presidential self.

Hall et al. (2016) frame their analysis of Trump's gestures in terms of how it contributes to the political figure's entertainment value, and how the allure of Trump's hyperbolic style – both its linguistic and gestural features – reflects changing values associated with late capitalism, like the rise of style over substance and the mutual permeability of elite and popular culture that has accompanied a dramatic increase in the number of channels, platforms, and modalities through which we consume politics (p. 2). Donald Trump as celebrity and spectacle, they argue, is entertaining to everyone – supporters and detractors alike – in the sense that he provides comedic relief regardless of whether you're laughing with him or at him.

A key element of Trump's highly crafted, idiosyncratic, and immediately recognizable personal style, Hall et al. claim, is his dramatic use of gesture. Building on the work of Erving Goffman (1959, 1974) and focusing in particular on his use of iconic, imitative gestures that caricature his political opponents and various others (e.g., a disabled journalist, Mexicans), they emphasize that these comedic gestural stylizations serve the function of a certain type of carnivalesque humor that bolster Trump as a comedic reality star-cum-politician in that they allow the politician to harshly intone his disalignment with these various others while lowering the potential for critical reaction to his embodied performances. Whether or not audiences consider his caricatures in good taste, the authors argue that viewers must suspend their critical lens in order to engage in this particular type of comedic performance. To repeat their words, "It is hard to critique a clown: we are too busy laughing" (3).

Hall et al. provide a detailed description of several iconic gestures that Donald Trump employs in his speeches. First, he frequently embraces the "pistol hand" gesture, a metonymic gesture and intertextual reference to his own gesture from *The Apprentice*, which he unsuccessfully attempted to trademark a decade earlier. This gesture alone works toward building Trump's brand consistency and existential coherence by cuing audiences into the same tough, executive persona that he attempts to project as a presidential candidate by referencing his previous role as a tough board-room executive.

Second, Trump gesturally imitates his political adversaries, including Jeb Bush as "low energy" (by resting his head with eyes closed on prayer hands), John Kasich as "low class" (by depicting his slovenly table etiquette), and Hillary Clinton as "scripted" (by holding paper in front of his face, as if reading a speech). These double-voiced gestural reenactments of various others work toward constructing a self-image as an energetic, refined, and unscripted candidate who speaks for himself. Furthermore, these embodied cultivations of authenticity are also apparent in Trump's gestural imitations of a *Washington Post* journalist, Serge Kovaleski, who denied a quotation that Trump had attributed to him. In this gestural imitation, Trump flails his wrists to mock the reporter's physical disability in order to frame him as "one of many 'incompetent dopes'" in the professions of politics and journalism. By contrast, then, this depiction is meant to construct Donald Trump as the only "competent" one in the field. This use of gesture is on par with Trump's use of constructed dialogue to construct an identity as the only competent presidential candidate, discussed earlier.

It is important to point out that when we examine how the various indexical meanings cued by Trump's gestural impressions line up with one another, there are striking inconsistencies: his self-projection of "refinement" via the impression of "uncouth" John Kasich's eating habits are surely contradicted by his decision to mock the physical disability of a journalist. However, as Hall and her colleagues rightly argue, this apparent contradiction is resolved in part by a competing indexical meaning: Trump's consistent projection of his own identity as the candidate who eschews political correctness in favor of "getting real" – a quality that reinforces his self-branding as the "authenticity" candidate. Additionally, it must be recalled that the pure entertainment value of Trump's comedic impressions reduces the potential for critical interpretation, while at the same time further distancing the audience from the target of critique. In other words, while viewers may find his impersonation of physical disability offensive in and of itself, this critique may temporarily take a back seat to their interpretation of the speech act that Trump is performing here (and one that Trump made repeatedly throughout his campaign): his charge that the mainstream media unfairly represent him.

While Hall et al.'s analysis of gesture focuses on Trump's reductive gestural depictions, or iconic gestures, of his opponents, through which he "[frames] their bodies as grotesque" (p. 82), it should be noted that even Trump's noniconic gestures – that is, his co-speech pragmatic gestures (Kendon, 2004) – contribute to the construction of his brand through indirect indexical means.

In watching the debates and speeches that form the corpus of this study, it can be seen that Donald Trump's pragmatic gestural tendencies in both monologic speech and dialogic debate contexts reveal that he exploits a contrastively larger and more televisually oriented gestural space than the other Republican primary candidates. In the debates, he uses two-handed symmetrical gestures more frequently than his opponents, who tend to use single-handed gestures to mark prosodic beats. Additionally, the gestural space of Trump's hands in both one-handed and two-handed co-speech gestures is generally higher in relation to his body – closer to his chest and head than his waist (although Democratic candidate Bernie Sanders is an exception on this front, as we also tend to use a relatively high gestural space). Trump's hands are consequently not eclipsed by the podium or cut out of close camera shots. Finally, his indexical gestures, unlike his iconic "pistol hand gesture," tend to be composed of open-handed configurations rather than a closed fist or precision grip (cf. Lempert, 2011), and Trump's fingers even tend to be spread apart as he gesticulates.

We can take Lempert's (2011; Lempert & Silverstein, 2012) analysis of President Obama's precision grip gesture as a springboard to see how Trump's contrasting pragmatic gestures work to construct a social type that is precisely the opposite of President Obama, or of any "establishment" candidate from either party. Lempert traces the use of the president's frequent use of precision grip to various levels of indexical meaning, relating to both the speech it accompanies and the speaker who uses it. In the case of Obama's use of this gesture, precision grip constitutes a discourse-focus marking device, indicating in gestural space where a point in rhetorical space is being made. Lempert then considers how the repeated use of precision grip comes to be associated with not only the speech that it accompanies but also the speaker who uses it. In the case of President Obama, precision grip comes to index the speaker as a "rhetorically sharp" or "articulate" speaker in oratorical contexts, thus contributing to the president's identity or brand as a politician, distinguishing him from others in the field in terms of his status as a "sharp" or "articulate politician."

We can use Lempert's mapping of the indexical orders related to the meaning of precision grip in Barack Obama's repertoire as a template against which to compare Donald Trump's use of a collection of large, two-handed, and open-handed gestures. Like Hall et al.'s discussion of how Trump's iconic gestures are understood by and appeal to both supporters and detractors, his pragmatic gestures can be analyzed along the same lines. Let us take as an example Trump's tendency to accompany his speech, and especially moments where he is marking discourse focus, with a symmetrical, double-handed, open-palmed, spread-fingers beat, either in the vertical (downward-moving) or horizontal (outward-moving) direction, at chest- or waist-level. This gesture contrasts Obama's signature precision-grip gesture at nearly every parameter. First, it moves through space without arriving at a precise destination. This is amplified by the double-handedness of the gesture; there are multiple points of arrival, which are sometimes even further apart from each other in space than the point of departure (i.e., when he moves his hands in the horizontal-outward direction). Second, the open-handed configuration of his hands give the impression not that he is trying to pinpoint an idea but is instead trying to "flatten" (in the case of vertical-downward movement) or "spread" (in the case of horizontal-outward movement) an idea. Together these movements recall the action of kneading and stretching pizza dough – taking something amorphous and putting some shape to it. Finally, the spreading of the fingers give the impression that he is combing his way through a large snarl, as opposed to the "pinning down" action indicated by the precision gesture.

To borrow Lempert's use of indexical orders (based on Silverstein, 2003b) in order to understand how such actions can relate to the creation of the politician's brand, we could say that these first-order gestural meanings may be reinterpreted and inscribed upon a speaker who is attempting to unsnarl and contain an unwieldy situation or idea through his speech. In considering these acts at the next indexical level, such talk and gesture may work toward branding the politician as the "antichaos" president; in other words, when Trump's indexical gestures are coupled with repeated slogans like "make America great again," "drain the swamp [of Washington]," and "law and order," they construct Trump as the big, strong, forceful Washington outsider who will comb through the current political mess the country is in and will restore order to American life.

## Conclusion

In summary, this chapter has investigated several interactional features of Donald Trump's idiosyncratic style of public speaking, including his use of interruption, constructed dialogue and co-speech gesture in both the monologic context of speech making and in the dialogic context of debates. Specifically, I showed that Trump's style of interruption manages to pull off a control maneuver in debates, allowing him to gain the floor away from the moderator and his opponents in a context where his performance time is limited by the strict turn-taking protocol of the speech event. However, the interruptive moves examined demonstrated that Trump's artful and entertaining interruptive style, and his stance displayed in interruption, worked to humorous effect, inviting audience participation and earning him further time in the spotlight, while consolidating his image as a tough, unapologetic, straight-shooting candidate.

In the analysis of Trump's use of constructed dialogue in speech and debate formats, I illustrated that his narration of conversations with allies like his family and concerned citizens and opponents like big banks worked to emphasize his role as a deeply concerned and uniquely competent candidate who represents the will of the people. In contrast, his use of constructed dialogue and vague references to the speech of others in debates worked as a persuasive device in the construction of epistemic authority and as a megaphone to reinforce the amplitude of his own positions by voicing them through self-repetition and through the echoing of others.

Finally, through a discussion of his co-speech gesture, and specifically how Trump's gestural tendencies depart from those of the previous US president, I illustrated how his large gestures come to index the candidate's brand as someone who will work through the chaotic state of Washington and clean up the mess with his grandiose visions for the future of America.

With an understanding of how these features work in the construction of a particular presidential identity for Donald Trump, we now move forward to examine how the candidate's talk has been taken up, recycled, and responded to in the mainstream media over the course of his campaign. We will do so through a detailed analysis of parodic stylizations of the candidate in popular late-night comedy sketches.

# 4    Parodies of Trump as metadiscourse

## Why metadiscourse?

In the study of language and political identity, it can be easy to reduce the study of sociolinguistic indexicals to the productive side of identity, assuming that a political figure uses certain stylistic devices that are known to index certain stances, acts, activities, and *in order to* construct a political persona that is associated with these qualities. However, it is important to keep in mind that production only constitutes half of the language and identity equation. As discussed in Chapter 1, the "partialness principle" of identity construction introduced by Bucholtz and Hall (2005) addresses this issue:

> Any given construction may be in part deliberate and intentional, in part habitual and hence often less than fully conscious, in part an outcome of interactional negotiation and contestation, in part an outcome of others' perceptions and representations, and in part an effect of larger ideological processes and material structures that may become relevant to interaction.
>
> (p. 606)

The partialness principle thus emphasizes the co-constructed and intersubjective nature of social identity, which is located in both – or more precisely, in between – production and perception. This concept incorporates what Johnstone and Kiesling (2008, p. 7) have described as the "intentional fallacy" associated with traditional methods of studying linguistic variation and social identity in which "features can be heard as bearing . . . meaning without having been meant that way." Johnstone and Kiesling demonstrate the problem of relying on production alone with a case study from their field research on the Pittsburghese dialect of American English and the construction of place-based identity. They show that speakers of one local dialect feature (monophtongized /aw/) are sometimes not aware of the feature or cannot perceive the distinction between the local variant and the supraregional standard variant of the variable. Thus, they argue, it is problematic for language and identity researchers to describe speakers' use of a local Pittsburghese variant as a claim to local identity. Instead, Johnstone and Kiesling argue for an approach to the study of language and identity that complements traditional variationist correlational analyses with measures of dialect awareness and perception tasks. I argue that the linguistic study of parodic performance can provide us with similar information that perception tasks do, because parodies highlight the social meanings that laypeople (rather than linguists) associate with the linguistic forms they hear.

In the introductory chapter of this book, I argued that in the study of sociolinguistic style and identity, once we move from analyzing the talk of "ordinary" people in everyday to talk to the study of language in the sphere of mass-mediated political discourse, the "partialness" balance is essentially tipped in favor of the producer, in the sense that a politician's language cannot be characterized by the vernacular, spontaneous, and interactionally dependent nature that we associate with the language of "ordinary" speakers. In any type of public appearance, the language of a politician can be assumed to be preplanned, rehearsed, and crafted by a team in a way that promotes both brand consistency and audience relatability. From this perspective, we can consider the language produced in any public appearance of a politician as an example of what Coupland (2007) calls "high performance," a concept that builds on Bauman's (1978) notion of verbal art as performance, in which he defines performance contexts as preplanned, coordinated speech events that are bound in space and time, and, importantly, a context in which the participant role of the audience is imagined as a social collectivity rather than as a set of individuals. Moreover, performance involves intensity, which Coupland further defines as involving several dimensions, including focusing on form, meaning, and situation, among others. Thus, the analysis of various types of intensity in language – like exaggeration of specific features and the extension and elaboration of particular discursive strategies – lie at the heart of the sociolinguistic study of parodic performance.

It should not be overlooked that the types of texts analyzed in Chapters 2 and 3 – public speeches and debate performances by a political candidate – can also be readily classified within the realm of high performance. It can be safely assumed that politicians place special attention on form and meaning focusing, attempting to maintain control over how meanings – and which meanings – are interpreted by audiences through the strategic use of particular linguistic forms. They have other means of control as well: after all, there is a whole media industry devoted to "spin." But when large audiences are imagined as a social collective rather than as a group of individuals, this type of control is also only partial. One characteristic of political discourse and of all mass communication is that it relies on the concept of the implied or ideal reader/hearer (Fairclough, 1995; Talbot, 1995) in the authoring of a text. The ideal reader/hearer is the target audience that the speaker has in mind when creating the text and is the subject position with whom any real reader/hearer must negotiate in order to make sense of the text. Real reader/hearers bring with them a variety of background experiences and identities that affect how they interpret texts. With this aspect of partialness in mind, it is important to keep in mind that while political high performance assumes a certain degree of power and control over the message, its interpretation is nonetheless as multiple and fragmented as its audience.

With this in mind, an analysis of stylistic features in Donald Trump's speech only provides us with a partial account of his political identity construction: the productive side. We must equally account for the receptive side, acknowledging the multiplicity of meanings that are entailed by the diversity of experiential contexts that his audiences bring with them when listening to his performances. In Chapter 2, I relied on correlational analyses that set Mr. Trump apart from the other Republican candidates and based my analysis of the function of his distinctive discourse marking tendencies on previous analyses of both political discourse and the language of everyday people. In Chapter 3, I looked at interactional strategies that Trump exploited for different purposes in debate and speech-making contexts; the analysis of gesture relied on contrasting his gestural habits with the only previous sociolinguistic study (to my knowledge) of gesture analysis of a US president. This reliance on an understanding of style as distinctiveness (Irvine, 2001) is also partial in that it selected certain other individuals as a backdrop for comparison. A shortcoming of comparative studies in general is that they can never capture the totality of meanings interpreted from any given feature or even a constellation of co-occurring features. Finally, I relied on only a few salient features in Trump's speech, potentially leaving aside others that are more socially meaningful to other hearers.

For these reasons, it is necessary to complement the study of language and identity production with a consideration of language and identity perception. While methods involving dialect awareness and perception tasks are useful for examining a singular variable in a geographically defined community (like Johnstone and Kiesling's Pittsburg), such a task would be difficult to undertake in the analysis of a national political figure's overall rhetorical style, given the diversity of his audiences, which constitute, at a bare minimum, the 2016 US electorate. However, given the importance of the office of the US president on a global scale, it is safe to assume that the audience of the presidential candidate's speeches has a global reach.

Examining explicit metadiscursive commentary related to an individual's speech is a useful way to not only glean a variety of social meanings associated with particular features of his style but also a way to confirm the relative salience of different features. In fact, in my analysis of discourse-marking and interactional features, I selected features that were also commented on in the mainstream media, thus integrating an additional perspective that vouches for the salience of these features. However, despite the variationist claim that only the most salient, and often most stigmatized, variables – Labov's (1972) "stereotypes" as opposed to "indicators" and "markers" – are available to metalinguistic commentary by untrained ears, advances in perceptual dialectology (e.g., Preston, 1989; Niedzielski & Preston, 2000) have shown that lay speakers can and do discriminate and associate a variety of social meanings with less salient variables at various levels of linguistic structure.

## Parody as metadiscourse

The concept of parody as metadiscourse can be traced to the work of the literary critic Mikhail Bakhtin (1981) and his theorizing of literary genres. In a collection of studies building on the Bakhtinian framework of intertextuality, Gary Saul Morson (1989) puts forth a conceptualization of parody grounded in the Bakhtinian concept of dialogicality. Morson defines the double-voiced genre of parody as fulfilling three criteria: it must "indicate another utterance," it must be "antithetical" to the target utterance, and "the fact that the parody is intended by its author to have higher semantic authority than the original must be clear" (p. 67). Without meeting each of these criteria, a text that is intended as parody does not achieve its purpose. For instance, a parody may not be understood as referring to another text. In fact, this is a mistake that has been made by international newspapers with regard to recent US political parodies: Fox News once used a photo of Tina Fey impersonating vice-presidential candidate Sarah Palin, mistaking it for the actual former vice-presidential candidate (Huffington Post, 2011), and a Dominican newspaper recently printed a photo of the actor Alec Baldwin impersonating Donald Trump (Croft, 2017) as a photo of the US president. This point indicates another important point about parody – that its audience must be encultured into the discourse in order to understand its hyperbolic and double-voiced nature. Parody can be understood as a subgenre of double-voiced discourse that has much of the same meaning-making potential as reported speech or constructed dialogue, a strategy discussed in

Chapter 3, given that parody relies on a prior text that it repeats to a certain extent, with modifications and different intentions.

I have previously argued that parody is a genre of high performance discourse that can be useful to sociolinguists because it provides us with a vantage point that overcomes the intersubjectivity blind spot that Johnstone and Kiesling (2008) describe (Sclafani, 2009). Parody can be conceptualized as a type of folk-linguistic analysis, as it is a text created by nonlinguists (though the creators are often specialists of language in another sense) that showcases the author's interpretation of an original text by hyperbolizing linguistic features that they deem indexically significant and attaching new meanings (often diametrically opposed meanings) to them. Through the analysis of parody, we are able to gain access to the indexical meanings that are perceived by audiences but do not rise to the surface through metadiscourse in mundane (everyday) performance in the way that linguistic stereotypes do. In addition, parody is also useful in that it tends to bring into relief the relative salience of variables by selecting and exaggerating particularly noticeable variables in the indexing of a particular social meaning in a potentially vast sociolinguistic field (Eckert, 2008). In some cases, I have shown, parodies even reify a sociolinguistic variable by rendering it categorical within the parodic frame (Sclafani, 2009).

I have demonstrated that the specific social meaning of a variable and its variant realizations is further specified in parody through the coupling of the linguistic feature with the exact opposite of its assumed meaning in nonperfomance contexts by analyzing two specific parodies of public figures, lifestyle entrepreneur Martha Stewart and US political figure Newt Gingrich (Sclafani, 2012b). In the case of Martha Stewart, the exaggeration of intervocalic /t/ fortition and final /t/ release, which has an indexical field associated with "goodness" at some level (Eckert, 2008), gets coupled with Stewart's bad behavior – that is, having been convicted and sentenced to prison for white collar crimes – thus heightening the comedic value of the parody by highlighting the indexical dissonance between linguistic form and social behavior in the parodic frame. In the case of Newt Gingrich, the language of a public apology he issued gets reworked in the parodic frame into the speech act of an insult. Through these key shifts, parodies can be seen as "indexical negatives" of style, shedding light on the "covert symbolic value" (Morson, 1989) or indexical meaning of the exaggerated features of everyday talk.

## The *Saturday Night Live* parodies

In recent years, scholars have recognized the importance of late-night comedy in affecting political attitudes and public opinion (Baumgartner,

Morris, & Walth, 2012; Moy, Xenos, & Hess, 2006; Peifer, 2013). As such, political parodies appearing on television are as important types of metadiscourse as are journalistic reports, social media commentary, and other forms of political commentary. In fact, parody may even be more effective due to its explicit entertainment value as spectacle (Hall, Goldstein, & Ingram, 2016) since it captures audiences' attention and engages them in political critique via humor. Throughout the 2016 election season, late-night television enjoyed record-setting numbers of viewers due in part to the anticipation of parodies of the US presidential candidates. In October 2016, for instance, just a month ahead of the general election, *Saturday Night Live* (*SNL*) enjoyed its highest season premiere ratings in eight years (Stedman, 2016).

Parodies of politicians on *SNL* in particular offer a unique lens for examining parody as metadiscourse as well as insight into the recognizable features of individual politicians' styles because of the show's long-standing presence and reputation on the late-night sketch comedy circuit. Currently in its 42nd season, the series has featured parodies of Donald Trump dating back to the 1980s, first played by Phil Hartman. This corpus of parodies, spanning nearly four decades and enacted by four different actors, offers us a window to look into a number of questions related to the linguistic features and evolution of the idiosyncratic linguistic style of Donald Trump. In this chapter, I will focus on the three most recent Trump impersonators – Darrell Hammond, Taran Killam, and Alec Baldwin – as their sketches double-voice Donald Trump as a political candidate in the primary and general elections. I assess which features remain constant when parodies of Trump shift from performing his reality television persona to his political persona, and the indexical functions and audience effects of the exaggeration of particular linguistic and gestural features of Trump's idiosyncratic style as his performance on the campaign trail is lampooned by these actors.

### Hammond-as-Trump

Darrell Hammond played Donald Trump on SNL for over a decade, with his early impersonations focusing on Trump as host of *The Apprentice* in 2004, up until he became a major Republican candidate in 2015. Even from the early impersonations, Hammond captures some of the current most commonly referred to elements of Trump's linguistic style, such as his tendency to use superlatives, his penchant for boastfulness, and his New York accent in words like "huge," pronounced with an initial /j/. Hammond also exploits nonlinguistic features like the use of symmetrical two-handed gestures and Trump's resting scowl face, something that Hammond has reported to have studied closely (Hammond, 2016). In one sketch dating back to 2005 (Fey & Steele, 2005), these exact features are even imitated by actors playing

Trump's three adult children, Ivanka, Donald Jr., and Eric. Maya Rudolph, who plays Ivanka in this early sketch, even hyperbolizes features of a working-class New York accent, such as word-initial interdental stopping, that are not found in the speech of Donald Trump or Hammond-as-Trump.

In Hammond's performances as Trump during the primary debates, the writers and actor rely heavily on Trump's characterizations and public perceptions of Trump's GOP primary opponents in order to showcase Trump's signature style. In the December 2015 cold open parodying the December 15 primary debate (Klein & Tucker, 2015), Hammond-as-Trump verbally spars with Jeb Bush (played by Beck Bennett), who presents an image of an insecure and flustered candidate trying desperately to stand up to an exceedingly confident Hammond-as-Trump, but he is succinctly knocked down by his opponent with crafty insults. For instance, Hammond-as-Trump emasculates Bennett-as-Bush by telling him, "Jeb you're a really nice man, but you're basically a little girl," and by declaring to the audience that Jeb's real name is "Jeborah." This choice of insults in this script plays multiple functions here: first, it highlights Trump's tendency to insult his opponents on stage; second, it relies on insulting language that is also sexist – a carryover from Trump's previous persona on *The Apprentice* and a quality that his language became well known for throughout the primaries, not only in his talk with other candidates but also in his talk regarding women in general; and third, it highlights Trump's interactional style on the debate floor, in which he manages to intersperse positive politeness strategies with insults. In this case, his complimentary preface referring to Bush as "a really nice man" functions similarly to the interactional strategies analyzed in Chapter 3 in that they allow Trump to come off as relatable and likeable on one level while he is engaging in oppositional and antagonistic discourse at another. Recalling the earlier analysis of Trump's self-branding as a "nasty" but competent response to the "nice" but ineffective status quo of American politics described in Chapters 1 and 3, this apparent compliment to Bush in the parody could also be perceived as a backhanded one.

In one of Hammond's most recent appearances on *SNL* as Donald Trump, he is a guest on the classic "Church Lady" sketch along with Ted Cruz (played by Taran Killam, who morphs into Satan midway through the sketch) (Klein & Tucker, 2016). This sketch plays on the distinction between these two candidates' identities in terms of their religiosity. The sketch begins with the Church Lady, Enid Strict (played by Dana Carvey, dressed in drag), referring to Trump as a "godless liberal Democrat" and then introducing him as "the tangerine tornado." These references already showcase popular perceptions of Trump – notably, perceptions about his true political leanings and frequent commentary about his skin tone, which has an orangish, artificially tanned appearance.

In addition to the stylistic features already discussed, like the use of superlatives (he tells the Church Lady her place "looks tremendous"), Hammond-as-Trump uses similar discourse-marking devices to those described in Chapter 2. For instance, he tells Enid, "*Believe me*, this is one classy funhouse," while making the "okay" gesture with his hand. Enid then corrects Hammond-as-Trump, explaining that they are actually in a church and suggests that he's "not a big church guy," or not very religiously devout. Hammond-as-Trump counters, "Oh I'm a big church guy; I'm there all the time. Sometimes I go, even when it's not church day. Mhm." This statement serves as an intertextual reference to not only Trump's talk about religion during his campaign, which was perceived by some audiences as superficial or awkward (Burke, 2016), but the many statements made by Trump during his candidacy declaring his affinity for various groups in response to being accused of bigotry, such as his claims that he "loves" or has "great relationships" with God, "the Blacks," Muslims, and "the poorly educated."

Enid responds to Hammond-as-Trump's awkward response by commenting not on its content but on his phrasing: "Wow. What a what a well put statement." In this sketch, the role of the Church Lady serves as the explicit evaluating authority of Donald Trump's language, style, and projection of political identity, while she also highlights what some perceived as a lack of earnestness related to Trump's remarks through her questions and responses for the candidate. Enid continues to talk to Hammond-as-Trump about religion, inquiring whether he is familiar with the Bible. Hammond-as-Trump responds again in an awkward and insincere manner, proclaiming his love for the Bible, but then as he begins to detail his favorite parts, his answer degenerates into an incoherent mishmash of religious and pop cultural references:

> Corinthians part /du/, Book of Revelations, too Genesis, too furious, which says, and I quote, 'Love thy neighbor as thyself, and like a good neighbor, State Farm is there' [audience laughter]. And always keep the Sabbath yuuuge! That's Moses. Oh, and the part where Jon Snow comes back to life, that's great Bible!

The exaggerated nature of the topic switching in this response, in which Hammond-as-Trump mixes references to the Bible with a popular film series, a slogan from an insurance company commercial, and reference to the television series *Game of Thrones* character, acts as the icing on the parodic cake in this segment. The absurdity of Hammond-as-Trump's answer likely recalls for viewers some of Trump's debate responses that were widely panned as incoherent due to his abrupt topic switching, while also revealing Trump's perceived relative lack of depth and knowledge not only about religion but also many of the other topics he skirted around during the election cycle, such as foreign affairs. Enid does not comment in detail on Hammond-as-Trump's response here; instead, the absurdity of it is left to speak for itself. After a brief pause, she just responds with her signature expression, "Well, isn't that special?!"

From these sketches we can see that Darrell Hammond and the writers of *SNL* borrow specific salient elements of Donald Trump's linguistic style and couple them with content that also critiques his perceived lack of substance when engaging in serious political conversation. Through this coupling of a grandiose style and a lack of content, the *SNL* parody plays with the idea that for politicians, style is substance, by inverting it to imply that Trump's style is rather a *substitute* for substance.

### Killam-as-Trump

Taran Killam's impersonations of Donald Trump, which aired in October and December 2015, are similar to those of his predecessor, Darrell Hammond, in terms of the linguistic and gestural features he exploits to perform the character. Particular to Killam's two sketches impersonating the candidate are his performance alongside his wife, Melania (played by Cecily Strong). Strong-as-Melania serves as an important resource for the discursive reconstruction of Trump's persona in these sketches, to an even greater extent than the Church Lady did in the Hammond sketches. The use of sidekicks or other supporting characters as a discursive resource in the co-construction of identity in parodic discourse has been described and analyzed in Sclafani (2009). The importance of supporting roles in parodic performance also highlights the importance of considering individual style in everyday contexts as co-constructed as well. Keeping in mind the principles of discourse and identity articulated by Bucholtz and Hall (2005), it is important to keep in mind that individuals never do identity work in a vacuum. Instead, they are provided *occasions* for identity construction in interactional settings. The same can be said for the construction of identity in double-voiced discourse. Furthermore, it could be argued that it is even *more* crucial for a parodic performance of identity to involve an interactional element so that the audience can witness from a third-person perspective – like a fly on the wall – the nature of the character's involvement (linguistic and otherwise) with others in conversational interchange, especially in what can be considered "backstage" contexts, because these interactions serve to reveal the inconsistencies between what we see in an individual's onstage persona and what the subject of parody's private actions reveal about their true identity. It should be recalled that theorizing on style, from Bakhtin's (1981) dialogicality principle to Bell's (1984) notion of audience design, has emphasized that all utterances occur with a recipient in mind. This includes all levels of listenership in the participation framework (Goffman, 1981), from co-present characters within the parodic frame to the co-present and televisually meditated viewing audience.

Killam-as-Trump's sketches are telling in that they use Strong-as-Melania as a supporting role in order to do the specific indexical work exposing the perceived sexist and misogynistic meanings of (the real) Trump's past utterances and actions. Donald Trump has been well known to American audiences for his womanizing tendencies since the 1980s when he made tabloid headlines regularly as a wealthy real estate developer for his glitzy lifestyle and marriage to Ivana Trump, during which he had a widely publicized extramarital affair, resulting in his second marriage to Marla Maples.

In the October 3, 2015, cold open, Killam-as-Trump appears seated next to Strong-as-Melania and announces to the audience, "You're probably thinking, 'Who's this? Another bangable daughter?'" This opening line makes intertextual reference to Trump's (then recent) statements objectifying women, including comments about the sexual appeal of his own daughter Ivanka. Throughout this skit, Killam makes extensive use of Trump's scowling resting face, or as Hammond called it, his "home base," to further the comedic effect of his language. In Hammond's words, Trump's resting face, consisting of a chin-forward frown and furrowed brow, is an expression in which Trump seems to be "weeding the negative thoughts out of his garden" and "converting everything that's strange and hostile into something that's really familiar and fun" (Hammond, 2016).

In Killam's impersonations of Trump, the resting face is exaggerated to an even greater extent than in Hammond's. Killam-as-Trump uses the resting face gesture as a form of punctuation, not unlike Trump's use of epistrophic punctuation discussed in Chapter 2. He pauses at each punchline, holding the scowl and leaving ample time for audience applause and laughter. These punchline pauses are significantly longer than what is required for audience involvement and applause, and consequently they allow the viewer to focus on his resting face for a moment of silence following the laughter. These pauses, filled by the facial expression alone, create interactional space for further involvement and engrossment in the visually salient aspects of Trump's style, and allow time for the viewer to wonder, "What does that face mean? Why does (the real) Trump do it all the time, anyway?" In the same way that Trump's gestures were described in Chapter 3 as being indexically mapped onto his political brand, Killam's parodies of the figure allow for further indexical reinterpretation. Through these reinterpretations, more subtle elements of an individual's idiosyncratic style become enregistered (Agha, 2007; Silverstein, 2003b) as carrying social meaning. That is to say, before these parodies, it is possible that audiences interpreted Trump's resting face as akin to his hair – perhaps unusual, but not crafted as a communicative device. However, when these characteristics appear in a clearly purposeful performance, they gain indexical meaning. Whether or not the audience has the same impression that Hammond described about "weeding the negative thoughts out," this pause allows for critical reflection and the potential creation of new meanings associated with elements of Trump's style that can then be applied when the audience next views the real Trump speaking.

In the sketch, Killam-as-Trump also responds defensively to criticisms Trump had received about his reportedly sexist and misogynistic language and behavior: "How could I hate women when I have the world's greatest woman right here?!" Strong-as-Melania, playing the dutiful wife, supports her husband's self-defense by reiterating his "loving" comments about women. She reports that he has said of other women, "She's beautiful! She's a 10. She used to be a 10, but hey, she's still a 7!" Such comments are in fact within the genre of objectifying and body-shaming comments Donald Trump has made, like grading women's beauty on a numeric scale (Mazziotta, 2016). Strong-as-Melania continues to provide support for her husband's "loving" ways, giving the example of how he gives her permission to go to the spa and go shopping when she wants. The parodic key of the skit makes clear that Trump's statements about "cherishing" and "loving" women have been interpreted by some as merely a façade for his misogynistic ways and his patriarchal attitudes even within his own family.

Strong-as-Melania then provides a "woman's perspective" in her defense of Trump's comments about Fox News anchor Megyn Kelly after the first primary debate, in which Trump made an allusion that Kelly had "blood coming out of her wherever" (Rucker, 2015), a comment that received ample media attention in the following days, with many speculating that Trump was making a euphemistic comment about menstruation. Strong-as-Melania says he was just "concerned" about Kelly, to which Killam-as-Trump responds, employing Trump's epistrophic punctuation: "**I love** Megyn Kelly. **I love her**, I think she's great." However, rather than ending his commentary here, as Trump was shown to do in the analysis of epistrophic punctuation in his speeches in Chapter 2, Killam-as-Trump continues, "But she's a heifer who's always on her period, and I hate her and I hope she dies!" By employing similar discourse strategies to Donald Trump's interactional style but through exaggeration, timing (in the case of his facial expressions), and betraying the original form and meaning of the epistrophic punctuation, the parody again highlights perceived inconsistencies in Trump's frontstage and backstage personas. By juxtaposing two perceived elements of Donald Trump's language – his penchant for repetitive, highly evaluative commentary and the misogynistic content of his language – the parody also highlights social perceptions that Trump has displayed inconsistent positions, albeit through a highly consistent style.

Similarly to the way the Church Lady highlighted perceptions of Trump's insincere claims about his religiosity, Strong-as-Melania highlights not only the perceived sexist language of Trump, but she also exposes perceived xenophobia in Trump's language. Killam-as-Trump approaches the topic of immigration policy in this skit by declaring, "Clearly, I don't hate immigrants," and then points to his wife (Melania Trump has immigrated to the United States from Slovenia). Strong-as-Melania then tells the story of how they met, claiming that Trump saw her picture in a magazine and called her up and invited her to America. When she told him she couldn't because she didn't have a green card, she reports that her suitor told her, "Screw green cards, they're for poor people!" She then reports that Donald has intimated to her that it would be impossible to round up all the immigrants and deport them, thereby making allusion to and neatly contradicting one of Trump's major talking points in his campaign speeches. Again, the explicit commentary by Strong-as-Melania in her supporting role here works to expose perceived inconsistencies between what Donald Trump says in public and what people believe he is actually thinking.

In each of Strong-as-Melania's supposed defenses of her husband, she exposes something about Trump's backstage persona that contradicts the public image he tried to cultivate throughout his campaign. So far, we have seen that she exposes his misogyny and xenophobia, and his claim that he would deport illegal immigrants. In the second half of the sketch, Strong-as-Melania makes explicit metacommentary on Trump's language by cleverly baiting her husband into admitting that he uses outrageous language as a tactic to gain votes. She first describes this as his communicative astuteness: "You know, Donald is so smart; he's so good with the media. You know, he know [sic] that if he said craziest thing [sic] he will go up in the poll numbers." Killam-as-Trump first denies this claim by telling the audience that he "speaks from the heart," but then Strong-as-Melania tells him that his poll numbers have recently declined, as she winks at the camera to let the audience in on her joke, and Killam-as-Trump immediately blurts out in response, "Mexicans are stealing our children!"

Next, Strong-as-Melania talks about her husband's brilliance and his specific plans, and asks him to explain them to the audience. Killam-as-Trump describes his economic plan in an exaggeratedly incoherent manner, with vague references to foreign powers and frequent topic switches, to which Strong-as-Melania responds by confirming his brilliance, explaining that she can't follow his speech because it sounds like "a jumble of words, it make no sense." Through this utterance, the parody manages to critique two elements of Trump's language and presidential identity at once. First, it indexes common impressions of Trump's habit of abrupt topic shifting as rhetorically ineffective and incoherent. Second, through Strong-as-Melania's self-deprecatory comment about not understanding his brilliant plans because, as she says, she's "not smart like Donald" and didn't go to "Hogwarts School of Business," the parody exposes the internalized sexism that some have suggested account for why so many women supported and voted for Donald Trump in the 2016 election (Moore, 2016). The character of Melania thus plays an important role in this parody because she allows viewers to hold Killam-as-Trump's language up for comparison on various levels: through her exposure of his backstage persona, the audience can critically consider what he says in public with what with what he (supposedly) says in private, what he claims to say authentically with what is strategized, what he says with what he thinks, and what he says with its effect on others. Furthermore, the parody critiques the way that some audiences have reacted to Trump's language throughout his campaign.

### Baldwin-as-Trump

Alec Baldwin has become the most popular and most acclaimed impersonator of Trump on *SNL*, and has become notorious for getting under Donald Trump's skin, as evidenced by Trump's frequent tweets about Baldwin's "unfunny" and "terrible" impersonations following the airing of Baldwin's performances. Baldwin has appeared regularly throughout *SNL*'s 42nd (2016–2017) season in nearly 20 skits as Trump, first as presidential candidate, then president-elect, and, most recently, as the US president. This discussion will focus on Baldwin's earlier work in season 42, in which he parodied Trump as a candidate, with special attention to *SNL*'s parodies of the three general election debates between Donald Trump and Hillary Clinton, which aired on October 1, October 15, and October 22, 2016.

In the October 1 cold open, Baldwin-as-Trump is introduced by the moderator, Lester Holt (played by Michael Che), as "the man to blame for the bottom half of all his kids faces," highlighting for the audience from the outset of the performance Trump's recognizably idiosyncratic resting face. Baldwin-as-Trump then begins with a metalinguistic announcement to the audience: "I'm going to be so calm and so presidential that all of you watching are going to cream your jeans." Here, the parodist alludes to perceptions of the first general debate that Trump's performance exceeded low expectations, especially based on the brash, insulting, and aggressive persona he projected and maintained throughout the primary debates – his vulgar reference ("cream your jeans") also solidifies these impressions of the contrast. It is worth mentioning here that Baldwin-as-Trump makes similar metalinguistic commentary about his intentions to sound presidential in the following two debate parodies as well; these instances of metadiscourse within the parodic frame allude to Trump's attempt to create a new type of brand consistency as the Republican candidate that differentiates his style as a primary candidate.

However, Baldwin-as-Trump's performance in this debate goes quickly downhill, and he resorts to his primary debate style of interaction. In response to the moderator's first question, which was addressed first to Clinton, Baldwin-as-Trump interrupts, "Hey, Jazzman, I've got a very presidential answer for this." Recall that in Chapter 2, it was illustrated that Trump uses positive politeness strategies and humor that create solidarity with his addressees in order to minimize the institutional turn-taking breaches such interruptions constitute in the context of debates. Here, Baldwin-as-Trump uses a seemingly similar style of positive politeness by beginning his response with the solidarity marker "Hey" and referring to the moderator by a nickname. However, by using a nickname with obvious racist overtones in addressing the African American moderator (he later calls Holt "Coltrane"), Baldwin-as-Trump exposes and draws attention to what some critics had referred to as the more subtle or covert racism in Trump's language. Later in the sketch, Baldwin-as-Trump returns to the exposure of Trump's perceived racism when he offers a new topic of discussion by saying, "See the thing about the Blacks. . .," imitating Trump's use of the definite article when referring to this racial group, which was criticized in the mainstream media and by some audiences as racist.

Baldwin-as-Trump captures several other salient characteristics of Trump's linguistic style discussed earlier, such as the phonological features associated with a New York accent, including "huge" with initial /j/ and voicing of the initial affricate on the word "China." In fact, when Baldwin-as-Trump claims his microphone is broken (an excuse he concocts for not being able to participate in the remaining 88 minutes of the debate following his first relatively coherent response), he tests the microphone by repeatedly saying "huge" and "China" in an exaggerated Trump accent. This is a prime example of what Coupland (2001) has referred to as the creation of "phono-opportunities" for the display of linguistic style in high performance. In this case, showcasing these particular phonological features provide additional humor because they are spoken out of context, creating a layer of absurdity at which anyone – Trump supporters or opponents – can laugh. (Baldwin-as-Trump later corrects McKinnon-as-Clinton's standard pronunciation of "China," telling her that it should be pronounced in his style.)

In terms of interactional strategies, Baldwin-as-Trump imitates Trump's interruptive style in the debate (though it should be noted that this strategy is not necessarily exaggerated) by interjecting "wrong" (which Trump did do in the debate) while Clinton is mid-response, although the parodist does take the illocutionary force of his interjections up a notch by saying "shut up" at one point. Baldwin-as-Trump also displays a similar straightforwardness in his responses to what was analyzed in Chapter 2 through the relative lack of turn-initial DMs. For instance, when asked by the moderator why his judgment is better than Clinton's, he simply responds, "Because it is. I have the best judgment and the best temperament." Similar to Trump's characteristic debate responses in the primaries, Baldwin-as-Trump answers a "why" question with a direct (albeit tautological) "because" answer rather than illustrating his good judgment with evidence or a illustrative narrative, the way that other candidates normally answer such debate questions and the way that they have come to be expected to do in debates by anyone encultured into the genre of political debate discourse. In addition to highlighting Trump's linguistic tendencies, Baldwin-as-Trump also performs some additional paralinguistic idiosyncrasies that where isolated to this particular debate, such as Trump's repeated sniffs that were picked up by the microphone in the original debate.

At the conclusion of the debate skit, Baldwin-as-Trump again makes explicit metalinguistic commentary in his closing statement when he announces to the audience that when he finds out all the details about Bill Clinton's extramarital affair, he plans to sit on his "golden toilet bowl" and tweet about it at 3:20 am. This announcement not only critiques Trump's extensive use of social media but also his habit of posting strings of late-night messages – a habit that received a great deal of attention and speculation in the mainstream media throughout his campaign.

*SNL*'s parody of the second general debate begins with extensive metadiscourse about the event and the participants by the debate moderators: they refer to it as the "worst ever" presidential debate; they take a shot of hard liquor before they begin, and Martha Raddatz (played by Cecily Strong) kicks off the debate by saying, "Let's get this nightmare started." As she introduces the candidates, after briefly consulting with her co-moderator about the appropriateness of what she is about to say ("Can we say this yet?"), Strong-as-Raddatz introduces Clinton as "President Hillary Clinton."

The second debate was conducted in a town hall style in which candidates sat on chairs rather than behind a podium, but they could stand and move around the stage to engage with the audience in response to their questions. The SNL parody takes the opportunity provided by this setup to highlight the nonverbal tendencies and interactional styles of both candidates. Drawing attention to the absence of a handshake between Trump and Clinton when they entered the dais, their parodists dance around each other like animals when they enter, and as their hands approach each other as if to shake hands, they both quickly withdraw and smooth out their hair.

Similar to the parody of the first debate, Baldwin-as-Trump begins with metadiscourse about his upcoming performance, announcing, "I am going to huff, I am going to puff, and I am going to blow . . . this . . . whole . . . thing," thereby alluding to post-debate analysis of Trump's poor performance in the town hall debate. He then proceeds to exaggerate similar interactional strategies that were exploited during the previous debate. For instance, when asked the yes-no question of whether he models appropriate behavior for kids, he responds straightforwardly and succinctly with no explanation: "No. Next?" When pushed further, he says, "I love the kids. I love them. I love them so much I'd marry them," making use of several Trump linguistic tendencies – epistrophic and highly evaluative punctuation, his habit of referring to social groups prefaced by the definite article ("the kids"). Additionally, this line makes specific intertextual reference to then recently exposed allegations of comments Trump made in the 1990s to young girls about dating them when they were older (Schultheis, 2016), which surfaced shortly after the much publicized *Access Hollywood* video leak of other lewd comments Trump made about women in the past. Similar to the parody of the first debate, Baldwin-as-Trump makes racist references, addressing an African American audience member as "Denzel" and replying to his question about representing all Americans with an irrelevant discussion about the problem of inner cities. He also very obviously shifts the topic of each question to attack Clinton throughout the debate.

Perhaps the most exaggerated element of Trump's interactional style in this debate is Baldwin-as-Trump's physical position on the stage during McKinnon-as-Clinton's talk. In the actual town hall debate, the camera captured Trump standing behind Clinton during much of her turn on the floor, giving the nonverbal impression of a show of dominance that mirrors Trump's verbal interactional style described in Chapter 3. In this parody, Baldwin-as-Trump not only stands behind McKinnon-as-Clinton, but walks back and forth, sneaks up on her, and then suddenly retreats ("like a shark" as the moderator later describes), while the soundtrack from the film *Jaws* plays over the interaction. It is important to point out that this multimodal parody of the candidates' physical stances provides a humor to the skit that is less critical than the intertextual allusions to Trump's racist, sexist, and predatory behavior that is accomplished through the linguistic aspects of parody. It is possible that bodily humor in parodic performance may play the same role that gesture-as-spectacle plays, as described by Hall, Goldstein, and Ingram (2016) (see Chapter 3) in Trump's own display of political identity. I will return to discuss the broader societal effects of these parodies and political parody in general in Chapter 5. It is clear, though, that the repetition of strategies exploited in the previous *SNL* debate parody have a cumulative effect, solidifying the audience's interpretations of the indexical value of Trump's linguistic style; additionally, it primes the audience and raises their critical awareness of language, which undoubtedly influences how the public comes to view the language of the real candidates in future debates.

In the *SNL* parody of the final debate, Baldwin-as-Trump resumes his exploitation of the linguistic, paralinguistic, and gestural features already described in the previous debate parodies, but in this last debate, in which Trump was questioned about his stance on immigration, Baldwin-as-Trump highlights the perceived racism and xenophobia in Trump's original remarks. The parodist makes intertextual reference to Trump's remark in the third debate that "we have some bad hombres here, and we're going to get them out" not only through repetition of his reference to "bad hombres" but through an extended sequence of Mock Spanish references in this sketch. Mock Spanish is a language register coined by Jane H. Hill (1998, 2008) that involves the mixing of well-known Spanish words into the English discourse of Anglo speakers in a way that, while it may not on the surface be intentionally racist, reproduces negative stereotypes of Spanish speakers. In addition to peppering one's vocabulary with Spanish lexemes, strategies of Mock Spanish also include adding the Spanish morpheme " – o" to words (as in "No problemo!"), affected Spanish mispronunciations, and nonstandard orthographic renderings of Spanish ("Grassy ass" for "gracias"). Hill argues that the selection of Spanish tokens in the Mock Spanish register, which include references to popular Mexican (and often Tex-Mex) foods and other words that connote Latino immigrants as festive, nonserious, lazy, and even violent, are employed by non-Spanish speakers in order to directly index a joking stance and portray a laid-back or easygoing persona, but through indirect indexical means, they reinforce covert racist meanings associated with Spanish speakers in the United States (1998).

In this debate parody, Baldwin-as-Trump proceeds to describe a conversation he had with the Mexican president, but can't remember his name and refers to him as "Señor Guacamole," and the president's wife as "Taquito," and their children as "chips and salsa." As I have demonstrated elsewhere (Sclafani, 2008a), Mock Spanish has been employed in other political parodies to expose the perceived racism of American politicians related to their stances on issues of immigration. Unlike the covert racism indexed by Mock Spanish in everyday talk, however, the use of Mock Spanish in a parodic frame alters the indexical meanings described by Hill. Rather than "covert" and "indirect" racism that could be countered by the speaker as having been unintentional, the frame lamination (Goffman, 1974) involved in the double-voiced discourse of parody makes these racist meanings understood by the audience as intended, overt, and direct.

This final debate parody starring Baldwin-as-Trump also focuses on perceived sexist and misogynist language uttered by Trump throughout his campaign. Baldwin-as-Trump not only repeats Trump's infamous referral to Clinton as a "nasty woman" in this debate, but when asked directly by the moderator about the allegations of sexual assault against him, he declares, "Nobody has more respect for women than I do." At this point, the camera pans to the audience, who erupt in laughter, which becomes amplified as the camera cuts to a shot of the planet Earth. Moderator Chris Wallace (played by Tom Hanks) turns around to quiet viewers, saying, "Settle down, entire planet. Settle down." In this way, the parody makes use of a variety of participant roles and communicative modes in order to not only imitate and exaggerate the specific source text of the third debate parody but also of Trump's entire presidential campaign, which at this point was coming to an end, as the November elections were only a few weeks away. Additionally, the parody also selectively reports and exaggerates reactions to Trump's language throughout his campaign, emphasizing critical reactions to his style and identity, and minimizing his supporters. *SNL*'s critical portrayal of Trump, and their portrayal of the supporting characters in these sketches, including Hillary Clinton (who is portrayed as confident she will win the election throughout the debate sketches), the moderators (who openly express dismay and incredulousness at Trump's behavior), and of the audience (who react with laughter and disbelief), reflect a particular interpretation of Trump's language and political brand, and one that, in retrospect, clearly represented only a subset of the US voting population. Media analysts reflecting on the 2016 election have even pointed to outlets like *SNL* and the circulation of similar parodies on social media as a problem that played a large role in determining the outcome of the election (e.g., Ingram, 2016; Sanders, 2016).

## Other popular parodies of Donald Trump

While there are many other parodies of Donald Trump that received a great deal of attention during the 2016 election, I will only mention a couple of them briefly here. Late-night comedians Jimmy Fallon (also an *SNL* alumnus) and Anthony Atamanuik, who at the time of writing has just launched *The President Show* on Comedy Central (premiere date April 27, 2017) featuring his impersonation of Donald Trump, both earned spots on *Time*'s list of top impressions of the candidate of all time (Hoffman, 2016). Because Atamanuik's show is so recent and involves impersonating Trump while in office, his impersonation will not be discussed here but would be worth in-depth analysis for an understanding of how parodies of Trump have morphed over time as he has shifted from candidate to president, and to understand how double-voiced discourse continues to be used to not only criticize the president's style and political identity but also his actions while in office.

Of Jimmy Fallon's several sketches impersonating Trump, there is one worth discussing in some detail, as it adds another element to the linguistic, interactional, and multimodal resources employed in parodic performance that create new identity-based meanings and effects in social perceptions of the figure parodied. On the September 11, 2015, airing of *The Tonight Show Starring Jimmy Fallon*, Donald Trump appeared as the featured guest. The opening act consists of a parody of Trump by Fallon in which Fallon-as-Trump is preparing for the interview in his dressing room. As he sits down in front of his vanity to comb his hair, the camera reveals that his reflection looking back at him is (the real) Donald Trump. Fallon-as-Trump looks at his reflection and remarks, "Wow, I look fantastic," to which his reflection (Trump-as-Fallon-as-Trump) responds, "No, *we* look fantastic and I mean, *really* fantastic." The two engage in a conversation, commenting that Fallon does not deserve to interview Trump, and the only one qualified to do so is Trump himself. Fallon-as-Trump then proceeds to interview Trump-as-Fallon-as-Trump through the mirror.

Fallon-as-Trump not only imitates Trump's voice quality, boastful style, and reliance on superlatives in this skit but also his gestural style. When Trump-as-Fallon-as-Trump responds to Fallon-as-Trump's questions through the mirror, Fallon-as-Trump continues to mirror his reflection's gestures. This particular separation of modalities across participants through a supposed mirror and the isolation of gesture in the parodist not only makes metareference to parody as a type of mirror, but it drives home the salience of Trump's nonverbal communicative devices that contribute to perceptions of his identity. It also encourages the audience to focus on this aspect of his style, potentially at the expense of his words. This is apparent at one point in the sketch in which Fallon is imitating Trump's gestures, and Trump transitions from a two-handed beating gesture to a one-handed precision gesture. Fallon uses the same hand (rather than the mirror-image reverse hand) to imitate him. Fallon seems to realize his mistake after a few seconds and switches hands, and while you can't see his face directly from the angle of the camera, his shoulders shudder as if he is laughing at his own mistake. This provokes extensive laughter from the audience as well.

The content of the interview alludes to Trump's inability to answer specific questions about immigration and economic policy in any detail, his proclivity for self-praise, and his habit of insulting others (with Fallon the major butt in this sketch), much like the *SNL* parodies described earlier. A key difference in the Fallon parody though is Donald Trump's participation in the parody. While several scholars of political parody and satire have pointed to the importance of the genre in the maintenance of public democratic discourse (e.g., Hariman, 2008; Kumar & Combe, 2015), it should be questioned whether this holds for the subgenre of parodies in which political figures appear on parodies alongside their parodist and collude in parodies of themselves, which has become a trend for US presidential candidates in recent election cycles on late-night comedies like *SNL* and *The Tonight Show*. The presence of the target of parody, which could be considered an endorsement of the performance, calls into question one of the three elements of Morson's definition of parody – that the meaning of the parody must be *antithetical* to the target. The collusion of the target in the parody can be considered to at least mollify and perhaps jeopardize the aspect of critique that is thought to be at the heart of parody. In fact, Fallon received criticism for his impersonations from some outlets for going too easy on his target (Bradley, 2017; Wilstein, 2017). The proliferation of political parodies in the age of social media and the Trump presidency has come to something of a tipping point, in which audiences are beginning to engage in the conversation about the purpose and effect of political parody, negotiating questions about when parodies are warranted, whether they succeed in achieving their intended meaning, and what effect they have on public perceptions of the target of parody. The indexical meanings of these verbal performances are also being actively negotiated in user-generated parody on a variety of social media platforms. As debates over the intent, effect, and merit of presidential parodies are still being hotly negotiated at the time of writing, this is still an underexplored area that deserves further attention in future research.

## Conclusion

In this chapter, I introduced the partialness principle as a complicating factor in the study of language and political identity, and introduced the need to study not only linguistic production but also perception. After describing past approaches to studying the perception of sociolinguistic style and the construction of identity, I presented the view that political parody can be seen as a type of metadiscourse. After highlighting findings from previous analyses of the language of parody, I examined recent popular parodies of Donald Trump on the late-night sketch comedy *SNL*. Darrell Hammond's impersonations of Trump capitalized on assumptions about the style-substance connection, revealing the candidate to use style as a substitute for substance in debate and interview contexts. Taran Killam's imperson-ations, which make use of the character of his wife, Melania Trump, to hold Trump's identity up as a specimen to be examined, reveal the crafted nature of Trump's political identity behind his "authentic" appearance. The parody also capitalized on Melania Trump's status as a woman and immi-grant, which are used to magnify interpretations of Trump's language as misogynistic and xenophobic, and her status as one of the few people who has access to his backstage persona to reveal the impression that Trump's language is not in line with his true intentions as a presidential candidate. Baldwin's impersonations of Trump, as he transitioned from the primaries into the general election, highlighted the perceived racism, misogyny, and xenophobia apparent in Trump's language. These general debate parodies also presented a skewed vision of the voting public's reaction to Trump as a presidential candidate, rendering the candidate (literally) universally laughable and hence, not having a serious chance at winning the presi-dency. Analysis of these and other popular late-night parodies of Trump, such as Jimmy Fallon's impersonation, however, suggest that parodists' capitalization on the laughable nature of some aspects of Trump's linguistic and gestural self-presentation may undermine the idea put forth by politi-cal communication scholars that political parodies can be an effective tool of political action and commentary, as they select only aspects of political identities that can be appreciated through the genre of comedy and enter-tainment, thereby reducing audiences' critical lens of interpretation through the selection and resemiotization of indexical features.

# 5 The sociolinguistic co-construction of political identity

## Where are we now?

The researching and writing of this book began in early 2016, when Donald Trump was still considered an unusual and unlikely underdog candidate for the Republican Party's presidential candidate nomination, and I write this conclusion as he nears his first hundred days in office. Over the past few months, headlines quoting the outrageous language of then-candidate Trump's tweets have been largely supplanted by headlines documenting the issuing and blocking of executive orders, cabinet appointments, and scandals surrounding Russian interference during the election and potential collusion between the Trump campaign and Russia. However, language continues to play an important role in the presidential politics. A series of early morning tweets by President Trump in March 2017 about alleged wiretapping of Trump Tower by President Obama set in motion an intelligence investigation, which at the time of writing, has shown that the president's claims were unsubstantiated. In May 2017, President Trump defended his firing of FBI Director James Comey, referring to the director as a "showboat" and "grandstander," which audiences found to be an either amusing or enraging instance of projection of Trump's own political identity.

Not only has the language of the president remained under scrutiny in the media, but his team of "interpreters" – his press secretary, spin doctors, and other surrogates – who are often called upon to provide metadiscursive commentary on the president's language, have also come under scrutiny and have subsequently become objects of parody themselves. Given that the consequences and legal ramifications of Donald Trump's language have changed dramatically since he has taken office, a study of current US presidential discourse would benefit from a variety of approaches in linguistics, most notably, that of pragmatics and speech act theory (e.g., Wilson, 2015). However, the analysis presented in this book sets an important backdrop against which we can compare and contrast Donald Trump's discursive strategies in his role as president, and beyond. The strategies, functions, and patterns discussed here can be used as a compass as we continue to ask questions about the function and importance of brand consistency and stylistic variation in the construction of an individual's political identity over time and through various stages of the trajectory of his or her political career. Furthermore, some of the findings regarding the multifunctional nature of DMs and interactional strategies uncovered in the qualitative analysis of one candidate's speech can be used as grounds for comparing the language choices and rhetorical styles of other presidential candidates, past and present, in the United States and elsewhere.

## Sociolinguistic style and political identity

The preceding chapters have taken up the deconstruction of the sociolinguistic style of an individual and the interpretation thereof via an analysis of parody. The analysis of the use of particular DMs and their functions at various planes of discourse structure – in the construction of textual cohesion, alerting the hearer to topical flow, marking of participation roles, and maintenance of interpersonal relations – revealed that Donald Trump exploits certain discourse-marking devices (i.e., "by the way" and "believe me") to a greater extent than his Republican primary opponents and other presidential candidates in recent history, which create a certain sense of individuality for his political brand.

As Johnstone (1996) has argued, repetition of particular linguistic features plays a host of functions in discourse more generally: it can create rapport, extend one's claim to the conversational floor, steer the conversational topic, or indicate verbal performance art. In her words, "there are few functions repetition cannot serve" (p. 175). Touching on the perceptive power of repetition, Johnstone also remarks, "When a linguistic item is repeated, we attend to it for the same reason we attend to pattern in all our sensory media. If we did not, the world would be chaotic" (p. 176). This attention to repetition is what political candidates rely on in their acts of self-branding. Donald Trump, who exploited repetition of a variety of linguistic expressions to an even greater extent than other candidates, came to be associated with social qualities indexed by the expressions he repeated frequently throughout the campaign, from DMs and regionally marked pronunciations to insulting nicknames.

However, it should also be recalled that other DMs were found to be used relatively less by Trump than other candidates in the debates. While the repetition of some linguistic idiosyncrasies were apparent to the general public, like his reliance on "believe me," others – especially the patterns that Trump exploits comparatively rarely – have tended to go under the radar of untrained linguists. This was the case with Trump's infrequent use of "well." If we consider these at the level of metadiscourse, we find that while an Internet search of "Trump believe me" yields dozens of articles, video clips, and quotes of Trump using this expression, a search of "Trump well" only returns stories about how the president prefers his steak. Returning to the partialness principle of identity (Bucholtz & Hall, 2005) discussed in Chapter 4, the disparate attention that listeners pay to what an individual *does* repeatedly versus what he or she *does not do* constitutes another layer of partialness in the language and identity equation. That is, a construction may be more or less conscious on the part of the speaker, as Bucholtz and Hall point out, but it may also be more or less consciously perceived. In the case of Trump, many hearers will readily point out his "straightforward" style, but it is doubtful that they will point to his lack of turn-initial "well" in debate responses as evidence of this same identity. Thus, this analysis has demonstrated the need for detailed and systematic qualitative analysis of political discourse in order to gain insight into co-constructed nature of political identity; we cannot simply rely on the linguistic commentary found in the mainstream media to get a full sense of how style works to a politician's advantage or detriment and how it works to construct a political identity.

The interactional strategies examined, on the other hand, revealed that Donald Trump used discourse strategies such as personal narrative, constructed dialogue, and interruptive behavior in ways that are not idiosyncratic, but are recognizable in the speech of other politicians and in conversational discourse more generally. Trump was shown to interrupt to a greater extent than other candidates, but by examining the language of his interruptions and the positive politeness strategies that accompanied them, such as humor, we were able to discern how he managed to present a likeable persona to audiences, overcoming potential negative repercussions associated with interruptive or uncongenial linguistic behavior. Through such interactional moves, Trump was also shown to capitalize on his well-known persona from his reality television career and entertain the audience, thereby engrossing them in his performance and lowering the potential for critical reaction.

The form and function of Trump's use of constructed dialogue in monologic contexts was found to be characteristic of findings from previous research on constructed dialogue as a discourse strategy in both political discourse and casual conversation. His recounting of past conversations with family, friends, reporters, and other individuals worked toward building his identity as a candidate of conviction, someone who left a comfortable and successful life in the business sphere because he felt called to serve the nation. This strategy worked toward building his existential coherence as a newcomer to politics. However, when the same discourse strategy was examined in debate contexts, a different pattern emerged. In the dialogic format of debates, Trump used self-quotation to amplify his own voice and his own stance on issues as a way to present his position as internally consistent and as oppositional to the stance of his opponents. When quoting others in debates, Trump remained vague on the sources and content of dialogue he was quoting. These vague references to past speech served in the construction of epistemic authority and the creation of his populist message. While these functions of constructed dialogue are not unique to the candidate's speech, their form and distribution across different types of speech events work in the construction of a distinct type of presidential self that sets Trump apart from his primary opponents and from what listeners have come to expect in debate discourse.

## The social and linguistic effects of political parody

The analysis of the *SNL* parodies of Donald Trump in his primary and general election campaign served to examine the perception side of identity construction. It was argued that parody is a type of metadiscursive genre that selects and exaggerates linguistic and nonverbal aspects of individual style in ways that expose the perceived dissonance between what certain sociolinguistic features have conventionally come to index and the qualities perceived in the individual who uses these features. An examination of multiple actors' impersonations of Trump revealed certain similarities across the characters created, such as Trump's use of evaluative superlatives, boasting, repetition, directness, and personal insult. The exaggeration of these features was coupled with behavior that exposed perceived inconsistencies between what Donald Trump says and what he thinks and believes, and between what is perceived as unrehearsed or authentic and what is actually a carefully crafted display of his presidential brand.

Furthermore, the parodies also co-constructed identity in the sense that they made strategic use of various others – Trump's children, his wife, debate moderators, and other addressees and audiences – to reflect and voice particular reactions to and interpretations of Trump's language and actions throughout his campaign. The presence of such 'interpreters' in the parodies plays an important role in solidifying certain interpretations of the politician's linguistic style; they also create space for the enregisterment of new meanings associated with stylistic features that are less salient in the target texts. Together, these parodies drew attention most notably to perceptions of the sexist, misogynistic, racist, and xenophobic nature not only of Donald Trump's language but also of his past actions and his proposed policies.

Additionally, the actors also manipulated salient aspects of Trump's non-verbal communicative style, especially his use of large two-handed gestures and his resting facial expression, to heighten the comedy and entertainment value of their impersonations. It was argued that the incorporation of carnivalesque renderings of the politician's gestural behavior functioned ambivalently: they created pregnant pauses, allowing for further critical reflection on the linguistic behavior of the character, but at the same time, their value as spectacle may have fogged over viewers' interpretive lens and resulted in undermining what many believe to be a central function of political parody – as a discourse of social critique.

## Looking toward the future

As I conclude this case study on the construction of political identity in a US presidential campaign, the reader likely remains with at least as many questions as they had at the start. There will likely be those who are underwhelmed by the scant attention I have paid to the *content* of the candidate's talk at the expense of a focus on style. Other linguists (e.g., Cameron, 2016) have argued that it is futile to examine certain elements of Donald Trump's style without paying attention to the content of his talk. This is of course true for any study of style, but in responding to this potential critique, let us recall the indexicality principle of language and identity: the social meaning of a linguistic form is made possible by the fact that in the articulation of any proposition, speakers have a choice of ways in which to encode their ideas through language. It is the paradigmatic selection of one option among many, and the syntagmatic selection of a constellation of features, that create a particular style. Styles are meaningful in that they contextualize the content of talk as emanating from a particular social position – one that is accessed via interlocutors' cultural knowledge about other speakers, places, activities, and stances that have been associated with similar language.

Given the time at which this book has been written, there are still several questions to be asked about the use of language and the construction of identity in the political life of Donald Trump. What elements of his style have remained consistent and in what ways has his presentation of self changed since taking office? Since the time period covered by this analysis of his style, he has grown a communication team, who are responsible for writing his speeches, relaying his communications to journalists at press briefings, and reconstruing his language when his administration faces critical challenges. The complex production format of presidential language and the intricate intertextual chains through which presidential language is mediated to the public open up a wealth of opportunities for further studies on sociolinguistic style and political identity. Furthermore, recalling the intentional fallacy and the importance of considering perceptions of style, there remains a lot to be learned about how different audiences interpret certain features when they are used by a particular figure. Answers to these questions are not only useful to sociolinguists as we attempt to fully under-standing the co-constructed nature of social identity; they can provide vital information to practitioners in the field of political communication and help communicators – both in the sphere of politics and in other professions – learn to use language in ways that effectively communicate with their intended audiences.

# References

Agha, A. (2005). Voice, footing, enregisterment. *Journal of Linguistic Anthropology*, *15*(1), 38–59.

———. (2007). *Language and social relations*. New York, NY: Cambridge University Press.

Alford, H. (2015, November). Is Donald Trump really a narcissist? Therapists weigh in! *Vanity Fair*. Retrieved from www.vanityfair.com/news/2015/11/donald-trump-narcissism-therapists. Accessed May 10, 2017.

Aylor, B. (1999). Source credibility and presidential candidates in 1996: The changing nature of character and empathy evaluations. *Communication Research Reports*, *16*, 296–304.

Bakhtin, M. M. (1981). *The dialogic imagination: Four essays by M. M. Bakhtin*. M. Holquist (Ed.), C. Emerson & M. Holquist (Trans.). Austin, TX: University of Texas Press.

Barrett, R. (2006). Supermodels of the world, unite! Political economy and the language of performance among African-American drag queens. In D. Cameron & D. Kulick (Eds.), *The language and sexuality reader*. New York, NY: Routledge.

Bauman, R. (1978). *Verbal art as performance*. Rowley, MA: Newbury House.

———. (2000). Language, identity, performance. *Pragmatics*, *10*(1), 1–6.

———. (2008). *A world of others' words: Cross-cultural perspectives on intertextuality*. Malden, MA: Wiley.

Bauman, R., & Briggs, C. L. (1990). Poetics and performances as critical perspectives on language and social life. *Annual Review of Anthropology*, *19*(1), 59–88.

Baumgartner, J. C., Morris, J. S., & Walth, N. L. (2012). The fey effect: Young adults, political humor, and perceptions of Sarah Palin in the 2008 presidential election campaign. *Public Opinion Quarterly*, *76*(1), 95.

Becker, A. L. (2000). *Beyond translation: Essays toward a modern philology*. Ann Arbor, MI: University of Michigan Press.

Bell, A. (1984). Language style as audience design. *Language in Society*, *13*(2), 145–204.

Bell, A., & Gibson, A. (2011). Staging language: An introduction to the sociolinguistics of performance. *Journal of Sociolinguistics*, *15*(5), 555–572.

Blakemore, D. (2001). Discourse and relevance theory. In D. Tannen, H. E. Hamilton, & D. Schiffrin (Eds.), *The handbook of discourse analysis* (pp. 100–118). Malden, MA: Wiley.

Bourdieu, P. (1991). *Language and symbolic power*. Cambridge: Polity Press.

Bradley, L. (2017, January 31). Can Jimmy Fallon's Trump impersonation survive a Trump presidency? *Vanity Fair*. Retrieved from www.vanityfair.com/hollywood/2017/01/jimmy-fallon-donald-trump-impression-muslim-ban. Accessed May 12, 2017.

Britain, D. (1992). Linguistic change in intonation: The use of high rising terminals in New Zealand English. *Language Variation and Change, 4*(1), 77–104.

Brooks, D. (2016, March 29). The sexual politics of 2016. *The New York Times*. Retrieved from www.nytimes.com/2016/03/29/opinion/the-sexual-politics-of-2016.html. Accessed May 10, 2017.

Brown, P., & Levinson, S. C. (1987). *Politeness: Some universals in language usage*. Cambridge: Cambridge University Press.

Bucholtz, M., & Hall, K. (2005). Identity and interaction: A sociocultural linguistic approach. *Discourse Studies, 7*(4–5), 585–614.

Bump, P. (2016, June 8). Trump got the most GOP votes ever – both for and against him – and other fun facts. *The Washington Post*. Retrieved from www.washingtonpost.com/news/the-fix/wp/2016/06/08/donald-trump-got-the-most-votes-in-gop-primary-history-a-historic-number-of-people-voted-against-him-too/. Accessed May 10, 2017.

Burke, D. (2016, October 24). The guilt-free gospel of Donald Trump. *CNN*. Retrieved from www.cnn.com/2016/10/21/politics/trump-religion-gospel/. Accessed May 12, 2017.

Cameron, D. (2016, October 28). *Donald Trump talks like a woman (and the moon is made of green cheese)*. [Web log comment]. Retrieved from https://debuk.wordpress.com/2016/10/28/donald-trump-talks-like-a-woman-and-the-moon-is-made-of-green-cheese/. Accessed May 10, 2017.

Chafe, W. (1985). Linguistic differences produced by differences between speaking and writing. *Literacy, Language, and Learning: The Nature and Consequences of Reading and Writing, 105*, 23.

———. (1994). *Discourse, consciousness and time: The flow and displacement of time and consciousness in speaking and writing*. Chicago, IL: University of Chicago Press.

Chafe, W., & Tannen, D. (1987). The relation between written and spoken language. *Annual Review of Anthropology, 16*, 383–407.

Chavez, P., Stracqualursi, V., & Keneally, M. (2016, October 26). A history of the Donald Trump-Megyn Kelly feud. *ABC News*. Retrieved from http://abcnews.go.com/Politics/history-donald-trump-megyn-kelly-feud/story?id=36526503. Accessed May 16, 2017.

Clayman, S. E. (2001). Answers and evasions. *Language in Society, 30*(3), 403–442.

Conway, B. A., Kenski, K., & Wang, D. (2013). Twitter use by presidential primary candidates during the 2012 campaign. *American Behavioral Scientist, 57*(11), 1596–1610.

Coupland, N. (2001). Language, situation, and relational self: Theorizing dialect-style in sociolinguistics. In P. Eckert & J. Rickford (Eds.), *Style and sociolinguistic variation* (pp. 185–210). New York, NY: Cambridge University Press.

———. (2007). *Style: Language variation and identity*. Cambridge: Cambridge University Press.

Croft, J. (2017, February 13). Newspaper apologizes after mistaking Alec Baldwin for President Trump. *CNN Politics*. Retrieved from www.cnn.com/2017/02/12/politics/dominican-newspaper-confuses-baldwin-trump/. Accessed May 12, 2017.

De Fina, A., Schiffrin, D., & Bamberg, M. (Eds.) (2006). *Discourse and identity*. New York, NY: Cambridge University Press.

Duranti, A. (2006). Narrating the political self in a campaign for US Congress. *Language in Society*, *35*(4), 467–497.

Eckert, P. (2000). *Linguistic variation as social practice*. Malden, MA: Blackwell.

———. (2008). Variation and the indexical field. *Journal of Sociolinguistics*, *12*(4), 453–476.

———. (2012). Three waves of variation study: The emergence of meaning in the study of sociolinguistic variation. *Annual review of Anthropology*, *41*, 87–100.

Eckert, P., & Rickford, J. R. (Eds.) (2001). *Style and sociolinguistic variation*. New York, NY: Cambridge University Press.

Englebretson, R. (Ed.) (2007). *Stancetaking in discourse: Subjectivity, evaluation, interaction*. Philadelphia, PA: John Benjamins.

Evans, H. K., Cordova, V., & Sipole, S. (2014). Twitter style: An analysis of how house candidates used Twitter in their 2012 campaigns. *PS: Political Science & Politics*, *47*(2), 454–462.

Fahnestock, J. (2011). *Rhetorical style: The uses of language in persuasion*. New York, NY: Oxford University Press.

Fairclough, N (1992). *Discourse and social change*. Cambridge: Polity Press.

———. (1995). *Media discourse*. London: E. Arnold.

Fey, T., & Steele, A. (Writers), & McCarthey-Miller, B. (Director). (2005, February 5). Season 30, Episode 11. [Television series episode.] In L. Michaels (Producer), *Saturday night live*. New York, NY: NBC Studios.

Fox Tree, J. E., & Schrock, J. C. (2002). Basic meanings of you know and I mean. *Journal of Pragmatics*, *34*(6), 727–747.

Fraser, B. (1999). What are discourse markers? *Journal of Pragmatics*, *31*(7), 931–952.

Fuller, J. M. (2003). The influence of speaker roles on discourse marker use. *Journal of Pragmatics*, *35*(1), 23–45.

Gal, S., & Irvine, J. T. (2000). Language ideology and linguistic differentiation. In P. Kroskrity (Ed.), *Regimes of language* (pp. 35–84). Santa Fe, NM: School of American Research Press.

Georgakopoulou, A. (2007). *Small stories, interaction and identities*. Amsterdam: John Benjamins.

Goffman, E. (1959). *The presentation of self in everyday life*. New York, NY: Doubleday.

————. (1974). *Frame analysis: An essay on the organization of experience*. Cambridge, MA: Harvard University Press.

————. (1981). *Forms of talk*. Philadelphia: University of Pennsylvania Press.

Gordon, C. (2004). 'Al Gore's our guy': Linguistically constructing a family political identity. *Discourse & Society, 15*(5), 607–631.

Gordon, C., Tannen, D., & Sacknovitz, A. (2007). A working father: One man's talk about parenting at work. In D. Tannen, S. Kendall, & C. Gordon (Eds.), *Family talk: Discourse and identity in four American families* (pp. 195–233). New York, NY: Oxford University Press.

Gumperz, J. J. (1982). *Discourse strategies* (Vol. 1). Cambridge: Cambridge University Press.

Guo, J. (2016, February 9). Donald Trump's accent, explained. *The Washington Post*. Retrieved from www.washingtonpost.com/news/wonk/wp/2016/02/09/whats-up-with-donald-trumps-voice/. Accessed May 10, 2017.

Guy, G., & Vonwiller, J. (1984). The meaning of an intonation in Australian English. *Australian Journal of Linguistics, 4*(1), 1–17.

Hacker, K. L. (Ed.) (2004). *Presidential candidate images*. Lanham, MD: Rowman & Littlefield.

Hall, K., Goldstein, D. M., & Ingram, M. B. (2016). The hands of Donald Trump: Entertainment, gesture, spectacle. *HAU: Journal of Ethnographic Theory, 6*(2), 71–100.

Halliday, M. A. K., & Hasan, R. (1976). *Cohesion in English*. London: Routledge.

Hall-Lew, L., Coppock, E., & Starr, R. L. (2010). Indexing political persuasion: Variation in the Iraq vowels. *American Speech, 85*(1), 91–102.

Hamlin, S. (2015, November 23). Ben Carson's secret weapon. *Huffington Post*. Retrieved from www.huffingtonpost.com/sonya-hamlin/ben-carsons-secret-weapon_b_8616476.html. Accessed May 11, 2017.

Hammond, D. (2016, July 22). *Interview: Hardball with Chris Matthews, MSNBC*. Retrieved from www.msnbc.com/hardball/watch/darrell-hammond-on-how-he-plays-donald-trump-730116163677. Accessed May 11, 2017.

Hariman, R. (2008). Political parody and public culture. *Quarterly Journal of Speech, 94*(3), 247–272.

Heritage, J., & Clayman, S. (2010). *Talk in action: Interactions, identities, and institutions*. Malden, MA: Wiley-Blackwell.

Hernández-Campoy, J. M., & Cutillas-Espinosa, J. A. (Eds.) (2012). *Style-shifting in public: New perspectives on sociolinguistic variation*. Amsterdam: John Benjamins.

Hill, J. H. (1995). Junk Spanish, covert racism, and the (leaky) boundary between public and private spheres. *Pragmatics, 5*(2), 197–212.

————. (1998). Language, race, and white public space. *American Anthropologist, 100*(3), 680–689.

————. (2008). *The everyday language of white racism*. Malden, MA: Wiley-Blackwell.

Hodges, A. (2011). *The "War on Terror" narrative: Discourse and intertextuality in the construction and contestation of sociopolitical reality*. New York, NY: Oxford University Press.

Hoffman, A. (2016, September 28). The 9 greatest Donald Trump and Hillary Clinton impressions of all time. *Time*. Retrieved from http://time.com/4451557/donald-trump-hillary-clinton-impressions/. Accessed May 17, 2017.

*Huffington Post*. (2011, June 6). Fox News shows Tina Fey in on-screen graphic for Sarah Palin. Retrieved from www.huffingtonpost.com/2011/06/06/fox-news-tina-fey-sarah-palin_n_871604.html. Accessed May 12, 2017.

Ingram, M. (2016, November 9). Here's why the media failed to predict a Donald Trump victory. *Fortune*. Retrieved from http://fortune.com/2016/11/09/media-trump-failure/. Accessed May 15, 2017.

Irvine, J. (2001). "Style" as distinctiveness: The culture and ideology of linguistic differentiation. In P. Eckert & J. Rickford (Eds.), *Style and sociolinguistic variation* (pp. 21–43). New York, NY: Cambridge University Press.

Jaffe, A. (2009). *Stance: Sociolinguistic perspectives*. New York, NY: Oxford University Press.

Jamieson, K. H. (1995). *Beyond the double bind: Women and leadership*. New York, NY: Oxford University Press.

Johnstone, B. (1996). *The linguistic individual: Self-expression in language and linguistics*. New York, NY: Oxford University Press.

———. (2008). *Discourse analysis*. Malden, MA: Blackwell.

Johnstone, B., & Kiesling, S. F. (2008). Indexicality and experience: Exploring the meanings of /aw/-monophthongization in Pittsburgh. *Journal of Sociolinguistics*, *12*(1), 5–33.

Jucker, A. H. (1993). The discourse marker well: A relevance-theoretical account. *Journal of Pragmatics*, *19*(5), 435–452.

Jucker, A. H., & Smith, S. W. (1998). And people just you know like 'wow': Discourse markers as negotiating strategies. In A. H. Jucker & Y. Ziv (Eds.), *Discourse markers: Descriptions and theory* (pp. 171–201). Philadelphia, PA: John Benjamins.

Jucker, A. H., & Ziv, Y. (Eds.) (1998). *Discourse markers: Descriptions and theory* (Vol. 57). Philadelphia, PA: John Benjamins.

Kantrowitz, A. (2012, December). 2012 wasn't the "Twitter election," but watch out for 2016. *Mediashift*. Retrieved from http://mediashift.org/2012/12/2012-wasnt-the-twitter-election-but-watch-out-for-2016348/. Accessed May 10, 2017.

Kelly, C., & Schneider, S. (2016) (Writers), & King, D. R. (Director). (2016, October 1). Season 42, Episode 1. [Television series episode]. In L. Michaels (Producer), *Saturday night live*. New York, NY: NBC Studios.

———. (2016, October 15). Season 42, Episode 3. [Television series episode]. In L. Michaels (Producer), *Saturday night live*. New York, NY: NBC Studios.

———. (2016, October 22). Season 42, Episode 4. [Television series episode]. In L. Michaels (Producer), *Saturday night live*. New York, NY: NBC Studios.

Kendall, S. (2006). Positioning the female voice within work and family. In J. Baxter (Ed.), *Speaking out: The female voice in public contexts* (pp. 179–197). London: Palgrave Macmillan.

Kendon, A. (2004). *Gesture: Visible action as utterance*. New York, NY: Cambridge University Press.

Klein, R., & Tucker, B. (Writers), & King, D. R. (Director). (2015, October 3). Season 41, Episode 9. [Television series episode]. In L. Michaels (Producer), *Saturday Night Live*. New York, NY: NBC Studios.

———. (2015, December 5). Season 41, Episode 9. [Television series episode]. In L. Michaels (Producer), *Saturday Night Live*. New York, NY: NBC Studios.

———. (2015, December 19). Season 41, Episode 9. [Television series episode]. In L. Michaels (Producer), *Saturday Night Live*. New York, NY: NBC Studios.

———. (2016, May 7). Season 41, Episode 19. [Television series episode].

Kumar, S., & Combe, K. (2015). Political parody and satire as subversive speech in the global digital sphere. *International Communication Gazette*, *77*(3), 211–214.

Kuo, S. H. (2001). Reported speech in Chinese political discourse. *Discourse Studies*, *3*(2), 181–202.

Labov, W. (1972). *Sociolinguistic patterns*. Philadelphia, PA: University of Pennsylvania Press.

Lakoff, R. T. (1973). *The logic of politeness: Minding your p's and q's*. Papers from the Ninth Regional Meeting, Chicago Linguistic Society, Chicago, 292–305.

———. (2000). *The language war*. Berkeley, CA: The University of California Press.

———. (2004) [1975]). Language and woman's place. In M. Bucholtz (Ed.), *Language and woman's place: Text and commentaries*. New York, NY: Oxford University Press.

———. (2005). The politics of nice. *Journal of Politeness Research*, *1*(2), 173–191.

———. (2016, February 6). *No excuses, please!* [Web log comment]. Retrieved from https://robinlakoff.com/language/no-excuses-please/. Accessed May 10, 2017.

———. (2016, April 6). *Donald Trump, the poet*. [Web log comment]. Retrieved from https://robinlakoff.com/language/donald-trump-the-poet/#more-220. Accessed May 10, 2017.

Lauerbach, G. (2006). Discourse representation in political interviews: The construction of identities and relations through voicing and ventriloquizing. *Journal of Pragmatics*, *38*(2), 196–215.

Lave, J., & Wenger, E. (1991). *Situated learning: Legitimate peripheral participation*. Cambridge: Cambridge University Press.

Lempert, M. (2009). On 'flip-flopping': Branded stance-taking in US electoral politics. *Journal of Sociolinguistics*, *13*(2), 223–248.

———. (2011). Barack Obama, being sharp: Indexical order in the pragmatics of precision-grip gesture. *Gesture*, *11*(3), 241–270.

Lempert, M., & Silverstein, M. (2012). *Creatures of politics: Media, message and the American presidency*. Bloomington, IN: Indiana University Press.

Lim, E. T. (2008). *The anti-intellectual presidency: The decline of presidential rhetoric from George Washington to George W. Bush*. New York, NY: Oxford University Press.

Mann, W. C., & Thompson, S. A. (1988). Rhetorical structure theory: Toward a functional theory of text organization. *Text-Interdisciplinary Journal for the Study of Discourse*, *8*(3), 243–281.

Maschler, Y., & Schiffrin, D. (2015). Discourse markers: Language, meaning, and context. In D. Tannen, H. E. Hamilton, & D. Schiffrin (Eds.), *The handbook of discourse analysis* (2nd ed., pp. 189–221). Malden, MA: John Wiley & Sons, Ltd.

Mayo, E. P. (2000). Party politics: The political impact of the first ladies' social role. *The Social Science Journal, 37*(4), 577–590.

Mazziotta, J. (2016, September 28). Donald Trump's history of body shaming: He rated female celebrities on a scale of 1 to 10. *People*. Retrieved from http://people.com/bodies/donald-trump-rated-female-celebrities-on-a-scale-of-1-to-10/. Accessed May 11, 2017.

McAdams, D. P. (2016, June). The mind of Donald Trump. *The Atlantic*. Retrieved from www.theatlantic.com/magazine/archive/2016/06/the-mind-of-donald-trump/480771/. Accessed May 10, 2017.

Meeks, L. (2012). Is she "man enough"? Women candidates, executive political office, and news coverage. *Journal of Communication, 62*(1), 175–193.

Miller, A. H., Wattenberg, M. P., & Malanchuk, O. (1986). Schematic assessments of presidential candidates. *The American Political Science Review, 80*(2), 521–540.

Moore, S. (2016, November 16). Why did women vote for Trump? Because misogyny is not a male-only attribute. *The Guardian*. Retrieved from www.theguardian.com/lifeandstyle/commentisfree/2016/nov/16/why-did-women-vote-for-trump-because-misogyny-is-not-a-male-only-attribute. Accessed May 11, 2017.

Morson, G. S. (1989). Parody, history, and metaparody. In G. S. Morson & C. Emerson (Eds.), *Rethinking Bakhtin: Extensions and challenges* (pp. 63–86). Evanston, IL: Northwestern University Press.

Moy, P., Xenos, M. A., & Hess, V. K. (2006). Priming effects of late-night comedy. *International Journal of Public Opinion Research, 18*(2), 198–210.

Murphy, L. (2016, October 11). Linguistics explains why Trump sounds racist when he says "the" African Americans. *Quartz*. Retrieved from https://qz.com/806174/second-presidential-debate-linguistics-explains-why-donald-trump-sounds-racist-when-he-says-the-african-americans/. Accessed May 10, 2017.

Newman, M. (2015, October 5). How a New York accent can help you get ahead. *The New York Times*. Retrieved from www.nytimes.com/2015/10/05/opinion/how-a-new-york-accent-can-help-you-get-ahead.html. Accessed May 10, 2017.

Niedzielski, N., & Preston, D. (2000). *Folk linguistics*. New York, NY: Mouton de Gruyter.

Norrick, N. R. (2001). Discourse markers in oral narrative. *Journal of Pragmatics, 33*(6), 849–878.

Nutt, A. E. (2016, July 22). Is Donald Trump a textbook narcissist? *The Washington Post*. Retrieved from www.washingtonpost.com/news/the-fix/wp/2016/07/22/is-donald-trump-a-textbook-narcissist/. Accessed May 10, 2017.

Ochs, E. (1992). Indexing gender. In A. Duranti & C. Goodwin (Eds.), *Rethinking Context* (pp. 335–358). Cambridge: Cambridge University Press.

———. (1993). Constructing social identity: A language socialization perspective. *Research on Language and Social Interaction, 26*(3), 287–306.

Peifer, J. T. (2013). Palin, *Saturday Night Live*, and framing: Examining the dynamics of political parody. *The Communication Review, 16*(3), 155–177.

Phillips, A. (2015, August 5). The 6 Trumpisms Donald Trump will trumpet in the Trump debate. *The Washington Post.* Retrieved from www.washingtonpost.com/news/the-fix/wp/2015/08/05/the-6-trumpisms-donald-trump-will-trumpet-in-the-trump-debate/. Accessed May 11, 2017.

Podesva, R. J., Hall-Lew, L., Brenier, J., Starr, R., & Lewis, S. (2012). Condoleezza rice and the sociophonetic construction of identity. In J. M. Hernández-Campoy & J. A. Cutillas-Espinosa (Eds.), *Style-shifting in public: New perspectives on phonological variation* (pp. 65–80). Amsterdam: John Benjamins.

Polanyi, L. (1988). A formal model for the structure of discourse. *Journal of Pragmatics, 12*(5–6), 601–638.

Pomerantz, A. (1984). Agreeing and disagreeing with assessments: Some features of preferred/dispreferred turn shaped. In J. M. Atkinson & J. Heritage (Eds.), *Structures of social action* (pp. 57–101). Cambridge: Cambridge University Press.

Preston, D. R. (1989). *Perceptual dialectology: Nonlinguists' views of areal linguistics.* Providence, RI: Foris Publications.

Real Clear Politics. (2016). *2016 Republican presidential nomination polling data* [Data file]. Retrieved from www.realclearpolitics.com/epolls/2016/president/us/2016_republican_presidential_nomination-3823.html?utm_source=hootsuite. Accessed May 10, 2017.

Rickford, J. R., & McNair-Knox, F. (1994). Addressee-and topic-influenced style shift: A quantitative sociolinguistic study. In D. Biber & E. Finegan (Eds.), *Sociolinguistic perspectives on register* (pp. 235–276). New York, NY: Oxford University Press.

Robinson, D. (nd). *Text analysis of Trump's tweets confirms he writes only the (angrier) Android half.* Retrieved from http://varianceexplained.org/r/trump-tweets/. Accessed May 10, 2017.

Romaniuk, T. (2016). On the relevance of gender in the analysis of discourse: A case study from Hillary Rodham Clinton's presidential bid in 2007–2008. *Discourse & Society, 27*(5), 533–553.

Rossman, S. (2017, February 16). Trump's repetitive rhetoric is a trick used in advertising. *USA Today.* Retrieved from www.usatoday.com/story/news/politics/onpolitics/2017/02/16/mess-fake-news-disaster-trumps-repetition-advertising-tactic/98014444/. Accessed May 10, 2017.

Rucker, P. (2015, August 8). Trump says Fox's Megyn Kelly had 'blood coming out of her wherever.' *The Washington Post.* Retrieved from www.washington post.com/news/post-politics/wp/2015/08/07/trump-says-foxs-megyn-kelly-had-blood-coming-out-of-her-wherever/?utm_term=.4d19778ba984. Accessed May 11, 2017.

Sacks, H., Schegloff, E. A., & Jefferson, G. (1974). The simplest systematics for the organization of turntaking for conversations. *Language, 50*(4), 696–735.

Sanders, S. (2016, November 8). Did social media ruin election 2016? *NPR.* Retrieved from www.npr.org/2016/11/08/500686320/did-social-media-ruin-election-2016. Accessed May 15, 2017.

Sarangi, S., & Roberts, C. (Eds.) (1999). *Talk, work, and institutional order.* Berlin: Mouton de Gruyter.

Sargeant, G. (2015, December 11). Who is the 'authenticity' candidate of 2016? Yup: It's Donald Trump. *The Washington Post*. Retrieved from www.washington post.com/blogs/plum-line/wp/2015/12/11/who-is-the-authenticity-candidate-of-2016-yup-its-donald-trump/?utm_term=.44d773e7c903. Accessed May 10, 2017.

Schegloff, E. A. (1968). Sequencing in conversational openings. *American Anthropologist, 70*, 1075–1095.

Schegloff, E. A., & Sacks, H. (1973). Opening up closings. *Semiotica, 7*(4), 289–327.

Schiffrin, D. (1977). Opening encounters. *American Sociological Review, 424*, 671–691.

———. (1987). *Discourse markers*. New York, NY: Cambridge University Press.

———. (2014). Discourse. In R. W. Fasold & J. Connor-Linton (Eds.), *An introduction to language and linguistics* (pp. 183–216). New York, NY: Cambridge University Press.

Schilling, N. (2013). Investigating stylistic variation. In J. K. Chambers & N. Schilling (Eds.), *The handbook of language variation and change* (2nd ed., pp. 325–349). Malden, MA: Wiley.

Schilling-Estes, N. (1998). Investigating "self-conscious" speech: The performance register in Ocracoke English. *Language in Society, 27*(1), 53–83.

Schourup, L. (1999). Discourse markers. *Lingua, 107*(3–4), 227–265.

Schultheis, E. (2016, October 12). More allegations, questionable Trump comments on women surface. *CBS News*. Retrieved from www.cbsnews.com/news/more-unearthed-footage-trump-says-of-10-year-old-i-am-going-to-be-dating-her-in-10-years/?ftag=CNM-00–10aab7e&linkId=29868172. Accessed May 11, 2017.

Schwartz, A. (2016, October 20). Trump relies on Mock Spanish to talk about immigration. *Latino Rebels*. Retrieved from www.latinorebels.com/2016/10/20/trump-relies-on-mock-spanish-to-talk-about-immigration-opinion/. Accessed May 10, 2017.

Sclafani, J. (2008a). Newt Gingrich, bilingualism, and "ghetto language": Online constructions of language ideology. *Texas Linguistic Forum, 52*, 131–142.

———. (2008b). The intertextual origins of public opinion: Constructing Ebonics in the New York Times. *Discourse & Society, 19*(4), 507–527.

———. (2009). Martha Stewart behaving badly: Parody and the symbolic meaning of style. *Journal of Sociolinguistics, 13*(5), 613–633.

———. (2012a, August). *Tim(ing) is of the essence: The construction of political identity in U.S. presidential primary debates*. Paper presented at the 19th Sociolinguistics Symposium, Berlin, Germany.

———. (2012b). Parodic performances as indexical negatives of style. In J.M. Hernández-Campoy & J.A. Cutillas-Espinosa (Eds.), *Style-shifting in public: New perspectives on sociolinguistic variation* (pp. 121–137). Amsterdam: John Benjamins.

———. (2014, March). *"Well. . .": Discourse management, control, and political identity in presidential primary debates*. Paper presented at the annual meeting of the American Association of Applied Linguistics, Portland, Oregon.

———. (2015). Family as a framing resource for political identity construction: Introduction sequences in presidential primary debates. *Language in Society, 44*(3), 369–399.

————. (in press). Performing politics: From the town hall to the inauguration. In R. Wodak & B. Forchtner (Eds.), *Routledge handbook of language and politics*. London: Routledge.

Silverstein, M. (2003a). *Talking politics: The substance of style from Abe to "W."* Chicago, IL: Prickly Paradigm Press.

————. (2003b). Indexical order and the dialectics of sociolinguistic life. *Language & Communication, 23*(3), 193–229.

Stedman, A. (2016, October 2). Ratings: 'Saturday Night Live' scores its biggest premiere in eight years. *The Boston Herald.* Retrieved from www.bostonherald.com/entertainment/television/2016/10/ratings_saturday_night_live_scores_its_biggest_premiere_in_eight. Accessed May 13, 2017.

Stelter, B. (2016, January 29). Who won the ratings race: Fox News or Donald Trump? *CNN.* Retrieved from http://money.cnn.com/2016/01/29/media/republican-debate-ratings-donald-trump/. Accessed May 16, 2017.

Svartvik, J. (1980). Well in conversation. In *Studies in English Linguistics for Randolph Quirk* (pp. 167–177). S. Greenbaum, G. Leech & J. Svartvik, (Eds.) London; New York: Longman.

Tagliamonte, S. A. (2016). *Teen talk: The language of adolescents.* New York, NY: Cambridge University Press.

Talbot, M. (1995). A synthetic sisterhood: False friends in a teenage magazine. In K. Hall & M. Bucholtz (Eds.), *Gender articulated: Language and the socially constructed self* (pp, 143–165). London: Routledge.

Tannen, D. (1981). New York Jewish conversational style. *International Journal of the Sociology of Language, 1981*(30), 133–150.

————. (1982). Oral and literate strategies in spoken and written narratives. *Language,* 1–21.

————. (1990). *You just don't understand: Women and men in conversation.* New York, NY: Ballantine.

————. (1993). The relativity of linguistic strategies: Rethinking power and solidarity in gender and dominance. In D. Tannen (Ed.), *Gender and conversational interaction* (pp. 165–188). New York, NY: Oxford University Press.

————. (2005). *Conversational style: Analyzing talk among friends.* New York, NY: Oxford University Press.

————. (2007). *Talking voices: Repetition, dialogue, and imagery in conversational discourse* (2nd ed.). Cambridge: Cambridge University Press.

————. (2016, October 7) The sexism inherent in all that interrupting. *Washington Post.* Retrieved from www.washingtonpost.com/opinions/the-sexism-inherent-in-all-that-interrupting/2016/10/07/9ccdd2a0-8c9e-11e6-875e-2c1bfe943b66_story.html?utm_term=.2679b70a9eb5. Accessed May 10, 2017.

Viser, M. (2015, October 20). For presidential hopefuls, simpler language resonates. *The Boston Globe.* Retrieved from www.bostonglobe.com/news/politics/2015/10/20/donald-trump-and-ben-carson-speak-grade-school-level-that-today-voters-can-quickly-grasp/LUCBY6uwQAxiLvvXbVTSUN/story.html. Accessed July 29, 2016.

————. (2016, May 24). On "believe me." *The Boston Globe*. Retrieved from www.
bostonglobe.com/news/politics/2016/05/24/donald-trump-relies-heavily-simple-
phrase-believe/0pyVI36H70AOHgXzuP1P5H/story.html.  Accessed  May  11,
2017.

Watts, R. J. (1986). Relevance in conversational moves: A reappraisal of 'well'.
*Studia Anglica Posnaniensia*, *19*, 37–59.

Wilson, J. (2015). *Talking with the President: The pragmatics of Presidential language*. Oxford: Oxford University Press.

Wilstein, M. (2017, January 31). Dear Jimmy Fallon, your Donald Trump parody
needs to stop. *The Daily Beast*. Retrieved from www.thedailybeast.com/arti
cles/2017/01/31/dear-jimmy-fallon-your-donald-trump-parody-needs-to-stop.
Accessed May 12, 2017.

Wodak, R. (2009). *The discourse of politics in action: Politics as usual*. New York,
NY: Palgrave Macmillan.

————. (2015). *The politics of fear: What right-wing populist discourses mean*.
London: Sage.

Wortham, S., & Locher, M. (1999). Embedded metapragmatics and lying politicians. *Language & Communication*, *19*(2), 109–125.

Zimmerman, D., & West, C. (1975). Sex roles, interruptions and silences in conversation. In B. Thorne & N. Henley (Eds.), *Language and sex: Difference and
dominance*. Rowley, MA: Newbury House.

# Index

For Product Safety Concerns and Information please contact our EU
representative GPSR@taylorandfrancis.com Taylor & Francis Verlag GmbH,
Kaufingerstraße 24, 80331 München, Germany

Printed and bound by CPI Group (UK) Ltd, Croydon, CR0 4YY
11/04/2025
01844008-0003